Alphonso Lingis
and Existential
Genealogy

Alphonso Lingis and Existential Genealogy

Alexander E. Hooke

Winchester, UK
Washington, USA

JOHN HUNT PUBLISHING

First published by Zero Books, 2019
Zero Books is an imprint of John Hunt Publishing Ltd., No. 3 East St., Alresford,
Hampshire SO24 9EE, UK
office@jhpbooks.com
www.johnhuntpublishing.com
www.zero-books.net

For distributor details and how to order please visit the 'Ordering' section on our website.

Text copyright: Alexander E. Hooke 2018

ISBN: 978 1 78904 176 7
978 1 78904 177 4 (ebook)
Library of Congress Control Number: 2018948894

A CIP catalogue record for this book is available from the British Library.

Design: Stuart Davies

UK: Printed and bound by CPI Group (UK) Ltd, Croydon, CR0 4YY
US: Printed and bound by Thomson-Shore, 7300 West Joy Road, Dexter, MI 48130

We operate a distinctive and ethical publishing philosophy in
all areas of our business, from our global network of authors to
production and worldwide distribution.

Contents

Contents

The fish trap exists because of the fish; once you've gotten the fish, you can forget the trap. The rabbit snare exists because of the rabbit; once you've gotten the rabbit, you can forget the snare. Words exist because of meaning; once you've gotten the meaning, you can forget the words. Where can I find a man who has forgotten words so I can have a word with him?
Chuang Tzu, circa 500 BC

Foreword

I was taken aback, when I received this manuscript, to see that Alex Hooke and I had been in conversation for many years, years during which I met him infrequently. The astonishment that conversation occurs between writers each alone without written or spoken communication and thousands of miles apart makes me see the marvel in that our thinking occurs in conversation with people of long ago and far away.

In a conversation one person isolates something or expands the field, queries, suggests, states; the other joins the path that appears, contests, affirms, casts light or casts shadow, such that in each one the thought that emerges is not mine or hers. What I found in Alex Hooke's book is not a commentary on what I wrote or a debate over it but thoughts that emerged in our conversation. These thoughts are before us not as my or his product but instead as insights that are now addressed to us, that lead us further. As I read this book everything stabilized as a thought in these pages beckoned me toward new paths to explore.

In Alex Hooke's book there is an exceptional sense of the weight of things. In so many passages he is not reporting statements or arguing for or against them but pondering. Pondering is not simply hesitancy before engaging in thought. It is stationing oneself among things, dwelling with things or events. Waiting upon them, as they make an appearance, present themselves, staying in their presence. Alex finds events and encounters from weeks, years ago, finds they have remained present, that he has continued to live with them.

Here thoughtfulness is not grasping and detaching things, not circumscribing their contours, not fitting them in classifications. Not observing, occupying a lookout above them or in front of them. Pondering is letting things and events weigh on one, is

1

feeling their substance, their weight

Here thought stirs in the sensibility rather than in language. The couple who have lived long in the Queensland rain forest, the researcher who has spent the winter listening to, contemplating the movements of wolves in the tundra, the carver in Bali who has brought into relief the spirits latent in different forest woods are so often reticent and slow to test words to speak of these things.

Thought moves in language and from language. The first statement of something taken to be true issues out of an insight. But henceforth one need only remember that there had been insight, without reactivating that insight. The statement is established, and one seeks to know starting from it. Thoughts too much thought no longer think anything, the philosopher Maurice Merleau-Ponty said. To think is to reawaken insights that were once tentatively formulated in words, and to seek insights beyond them. It is not to hypothetically take what is said to be dubious, for to really doubt something is to have encountered reasons to doubt it. But thought awakens, takes form in the move beyond the said and the known.

Alex Hooke moves restlessly from what I wrote to what I wrote in other places and sometimes long ago. He moves to what others have written, moving to many authors and also to things heard from friends or strangers. His thought does not stop on things I said or things other authors have said but always moves to assess, question, connect or disconnect. Thought is pondering but thought also exists in movement.

One is not alone and one does not think alone. There is understanding in Alex Hooke's companion dog and in arctic terns that scroll the seas from the Arctic to the Antarctic. José María Arguedas wrote of the wisdom imparted by an ancient cedar in a courtyard in Arequippa. Claude Lévi-Strauss wrote of small groups of Amazonian people who have amassed knowledge of thousands of plant species, most of which are toxic, and transited that knowledge exactly to each generation. To think is to be questioned, troubled, informed, perplexed by the thought recorded in millions of books. Alex Hooke remembers what he heard or overheard, knowing that every human being knows something nobody else knows. He makes me see that in each of his thoughts, and in each of mine, there are dozens who are thinking.

Thoughts are not only movements inching or leaping into the unknown but also movements addressed to unknown respondents. May the thoughts in this book awaken in conversation with readers nearby and far away.

Alphonso Lingis

Preface

Since Plato and Lao-Tzu, philosophical reflections and research have been initiated and anchored by dialogs, confessions, meditations, aphorisms, critiques, arguments, films, fiction, paradoxes and problems. They evoke comments and debates about goodness, truth, justice or beauty.

The work of Alphonso Lingis introduces two additional anchors. One is based on describing lived stories, especially the stories of others. Many of these emerge from Lingis's encounters with human beings from remote parts of the Earth. Others appear through encounters with local artists, family members or nearby friends. In presenting vivid glimpses into their worlds his writings revisit and reexamine familiar philosophical themes.

These encounters generally begin when meeting someone face-to-face. Despite the recent prominence of Facebook and social media where images of faces can be easily rearranged, to acknowledge someone directly before us or to catch another's eye remains a distinct experience. This becomes particularly noticeable when struck by the face of a stranger. No matter how sedentary we sometimes become, Lingis detects a nomad ethos that remains a human impulse. This ethos is often realized in ephemeral associations or collages rather than enduring collectives. In any event, by presenting the stories of others to his readers Lingis realizes his own precarious philosophical enterprise, as seen in his thoughts on silence and speech. These reservations give way to a more affirmative mode of knowledge via passions such as courage and laughter.

A second anchor introduced in Lingis's work we call "existential genealogy." This term is meant as a complement to the historical genealogy pioneered by Michel Foucault. Historical genealogy focuses on shifts and levels of discourse, the multifarious relations of knowledge and power, and the shifts in control and freedom amid the forces of government and expertise. One shortcoming of this perspective lies in its neglect of the visions or imperatives human beings actually experience while deciding to act or convince themselves that things do not have to be as they are. Lingis addresses this shortcoming with his as-if-you-were-there account of human beings summoning the courage, love or passion to address their own realities or singular possibilities. Many of his phenomenological sketches address a familiar existential endeavor—the project. Whereas Foucault quipped about "doing a history of the present," Lingis presents a "prehistory of the future." The project, as its etymology indicates, throws one forward. Many of Lingis's stories depict people telling of their projects, some ending happily and some ending tragically. In contrast to historical genealogy which begins with the present in order to retrace the recorded past, existential genealogy begins with the present in order to anticipate the uncertain future.

A significant thinker, writer or artist is one who pushes us to rethink our conventions and established beliefs. He or she also introduces unexpected approaches to examine ongoing disputes and controversies. Finally, the thinker initiates directions or extensions to conduct our own research in areas that strike our sense of curiosity or intellectual adventure. Daniel Dennett makes this point by encouraging readers to pursue their own research based on the writings of a compelling philosopher. In his view, "if you find them useful, they can be a springboard into your own exploration of the questions and answers that have been worked on for so long by so many thinkers." The case study and excurses that follow—the stories told and retold by pet owners, the birth of a famous musical group and the origins of basketball's first magic show—attempt to show how Lingis's ideas provide a conceptual lens for similar explorations into one's own experiences or fields of inquiry.

A caveat or two. This study will not elaborate on Lingis's relation to fundamental thinkers in the existentialist/phenomenological tradition. His relation and indebtedness to them will be addressed when presenting key themes in his philosophical story-telling and genealogy. Should attention to Lingis's work continue to expand, his books *Phenomenological Explanations, Libido, Deathbound Subjectivity* and *Sensation* will hopefully be reprinted in paperback and made available to general audiences for further study of his nuanced perspectives on Husserl, Heidegger, Sartre, Levinas, Merleau-Ponty or Deleuze/Guattari. Second, there is a prevailing and understandable trend among neuroscientists, evolutionists, environmentalists to situate humans as continuations or resemblances to the rest of the animal world. At times Lingis adopts this trend. On the other hand, in light of his stories, the photographs that introduce his chapters, the singular possibilities he depicts, there remains something distinct, for better or worse, about the human. Hence this study closes with a brief meditation on section #337 from Nietzsche's *The Gay Science*. It is the most frequently cited passage in the work of Lingis and envisions a humaneness of the future.

Part 1

Philosophical Story-Telling

Chapter One

Faces For a Philosophy of the Morning

Born out of the mysteries, they (the Muses and free spirits) ponder on how, between the tenth and twelfth day of the clock, the day could present a face so pure, so light-filled, so cheerful and transfigured — they seek the philosophy of the morning.
Nietzsche, The Wanderer[1]

Photographs

Which came first, face as a verb or a noun? A reader of a Lingis essay is immediately drawn to one of his signature features — the author's photograph of another human being. The images are a sundry mix. Many are close-ups of people's faces from all over the world. Before getting to the words the reader has already faced a Thai transvestite, a Mexican child mummy, street urchins in Calcutta, Ethiopian priests, Waadabe dancers in Niger, two cheerful Mongolian women, carnival celebrants in Rio, among so many others.

The relevance of the picture to the subsequent essay is not always clear-cut. At times, such as "Love Junkies", it is obvious the writing clearly refers to the individuals who appear in the photograph. Other times it is more indirect. An essay might begin with an image of a young man in prison, looking desperate, afraid or dangerous. Then Lingis develops a discussion about friendship and courage, implying that the photograph is of someone with remarkable strength and kindness when confronted with a sickly and vulnerable prisoner.

One photograph taken in Nepal shows a girl standing on a stone ledge next to what could be an older brother or her father. He sits in a crouch with a smile as she is talking and gesturing. With the mountains in the background, she is pointing outwards, as if there is a place she wants to see or must go. Lingis titled this chapter "Walkabout"[2], addressing the tradition of some cultures where young men and women are expected to leave home for a time. Admittedly, there are times I'm not sure why a certain photo begins an essay. Perhaps the photo presents Lingis's sense of humor, such as the image of the bearded old man doing a two-handed stand with his legs neatly curled above his back before a chapter titled "Murmur of the World."[3] At times the photo is simply striking or appealing in its own way without any particular connection to the essay. Skeptics have questioned Lingis's use of the camera. Rather than being an effort to present "the reality of the other," they contend that he engages in another exercise of Western privilege, particularly of a professional and successful white male. Logic students might recognize this charge as a possible *ad hominem circumstantial* fallacy. That is, one criticizes the position of the writer or thinker rather than the words and ideas being set forth. Skeptics insist on the relevance of this charge by pointing out the inherent imbalance between the well-off traveling author and the relative material lack of those whose pictures are being taken. The author occupies a safe and privileged position, able to escape whenever difficult circumstances arise. His perspective is hence skewed and his account selective. According to this critique, Lingis is hardly qualified to account for the actual worlds of the people presented through his writings.

Obviously Lingis, a full-time professor at a distinguished public university, cannot deny these personal details. He often intersperses his reflections with admissions that he does not pretend to be the ethnographer who "goes native." But he is not convinced that the *ad hominem* charge undermines his project. His response instead appears in terms of the gift. A general rule of thumb among photographers is to seek the consent of those facing the camera. Lingis abides by this rule. He also acknowledges his surprise over how many people appreciated their photos being taken in light of their never having owned a camera or even a picture taken of them. Being given colorful prints of themselves turned out to be cause for a local party in their home. The photos might be framed or adorned with pendants or flowers and become the occasion for friends and families to swap stories and indulge in food and drink. In Lingis's words, "Through the emanations of themselves retained by the camera, you will meet these people. They, however unknowingly, actively give of the visions in their eyes and the trembling of their hearts to you."[4]

In a word, these gifts are their stories, conveyed through a philosophical lens.

Stories

"There aren't any boring people; there are just boring questions," says Jim Nicholson, the first reporter to win a Pulitzer Prize for his obituary columns.[5] For him the axiom that everyone has a story to tell is quite evident. Finding it is the task of responsible newspaper writers. People die every day, yet in a large city like Philadelphia, Nicholson had to carefully choose which deceased citizens deserved a special feature in the obit page. He would quickly do some background research and then call or visit surviving family members, friends or colleagues. In six or seven hundred words he would tell the reader a remarkable story or two about the deceased.

An obit might cover Verne Meisner, whose talents with the accordion have placed him in five different polka halls of fame, or Buck Johnson, who first discovered how secretions from a deer's toe could be extracted so deer hunters could use it to disguise their human scent from the targets of their rifles. How many newspaper readers even know of one polka hall of fame, or that a deer's secretion could aid its archrival, the deer hunter?

Jim Nicholson had a knack and enthusiasm for describing the rich life of recently departed ordinary Joes to thousands of newspaper readers. With his eyes, ears and journalistic skills, readers learned about the idiosyncrasies and talents of a plumber who would fix neighbors' busted pipes for no charge, a grandma who was quite the bluffer at area poker games, or a local cook who everyone agreed made the best biscuits and cornbread in the county. According to Marilyn Johnson, Nicholson absorbed what people told him. "He would listen very hard to family and friends and find something in the person's life that was singular."[6] Before Nicholson, obituary writing ranked near the bottom of the newspaper hierarchy as it was assigned to rookie reporters and journalists nearing retirement. After Nicholson, the art of telling the story of a recently departed citizen or neighbor continued to flourish in many big city and small town newspapers. The stories inform and alert the reader to quirks and accomplishments of unknown individuals who nevertheless highlighted in their own way the canvas of human possibilities. Skirting the boring questions, Lingis takes the hearing and retelling of one another's stories as a departure point for philosophical investigations into the ideas about human conventions one has long adopted or respected. So he asks: "Will I speak the truth to you, Devika?" "How could I sleep in a bed in Calcutta?" "What law dictated that you chose to be my friend?" These are some of the questions Lingis poses in "Cargo Cult", the concluding chapter of *Excesses*. The reader meets several individuals in India, quickly learning about their relative poverty, the events in their lives, beginnings of a friendship, their cleverness and honesty, and their skills in deception and delight in a good laugh.

Throughout these encounters Lingis interweaves a dialog about traditional views on true or authentic friendship. Addressing the ideas of Aristotle, Kant and Hegel, he highlights the prevailing components of a superior to an inferior friendship, and human association in general. Friendship is posited as the ideal microcosm for a just and contented society. Unlike the intense fluctuations in erotic and romantic love or the conflicting pressures in family life, friendship is based on endurance, realization of one's *telos* or purpose, mutual recognition and reciprocity, wit and reason, and a stable sense of equality. Inferior friendships, those that depict a corrupt microcosm of a happy society, rely on mendacity, selfishness and unfair exchanges of goods. Devika opens up with all sorts of tantalizing anecdotes. Lingis at first seems skeptical. To disguise his own background, Lingis claims to be a journalist (but not an obit writer). Devika proceeds to tell him about characters and places he has seen in his young life that will surprise a well-read college professor. He recounts monkey cages where women and their children are prisoners or the local guru and his dance costumes. The reader anticipates a friendship where there is an inherent inequality. The professor can purchase a meal that would feed Devika for a month, whereas Devika's insights and speculations about life in India overwhelm the professor's assumptions on generosity, reciprocity and honesty.

Then there is Arun. Lingis takes a late-night walk to a well-known public square in Calcutta. Readily seen by passersby as a tourist and easy mark, Lingis draws beggars, lepers seeking alms, pimps selling English virgins or young boys, and emaciated mothers with newborns barely hanging on. Among them he meets Arun, who offers to sell some dope. They haggle over the price and soon reach an agreement. The dope makes Lingis quite sick. Weeks later he returns and by chance sees Arun again. There is laughter, as if a tacit acknowledgment that Arun outsmarted the professor. He then takes Lingis and us readers to parts of Calcutta never shown in the tourist brochures: vultures feeding off bits of human corpses, addicts getting a fix from cobra bites, lepers huddling under a dank bridge. The traveler will never see Arun again, yet their ephemeral friendship is marked by an unexpected intensity and insight not realized in the more egalitarian and stable friendships praised by many key thinkers. Finally, Gopal Hardilay appears, another chance meeting in India. Gopal entreats Lingis to nearby locales where they celebrate garlanded cows, smoldering fires burning the recently deceased, a bridal procession and the presence of Shiva the Destroyer. Readers learn of the blood sacrifice to Kali that took away Gopal's parents when he was an infant. There is the ghat or small boat where Gopal tries to find some sleep. The author wishes to offer a photograph of Gopal as a gift. In congested Calcutta, he can't find him. Weeks later Lingis returns and tries to find him, asking residents if they have recently seen Gopal. Word soon reaches Gopal that Lingis is back in town and they meet again. Gopal presents him with an ancient silver statue, worth enough money to feed Gopal's family for a year or more. This is not the friendship envisioned by Aristotle or Kant, where reciprocity and mutual respect are emphasized. It instead arises as expenditure or generosity. In Lingis's missive to Gopal, "I looked at you with wet eyes and realized that's all there was. Orphan boy you had given me everything you had."[7]

Faces

Face carries a considerable range of meanings. Despite the availability of social media and Skype, the live interview is preferred because we cling to our conviction that we can better detect another's sincerity and truthfulness through the face-to-face interview. The two-faced individual sparks caution as someone who is insincere or dishonest. To be in your face can be a provocative challenge or a superior's browbeating of an inferior. Facing up to the facts or the situation is an incentive to make a decision or avoid self-delusion. According to Angus Trumble, the face has been represented in an astonishing variety of ways. From early drawings and classic portraits to modern photographs and advertising, the face has been portrayed both as revealing or concealing who the person(s) actually might be. Can it indicate something about the person's actual life or situation in light of the image that is captured? How do the angles of the lips, the shape of the teeth, the placement of the tongue indicate a smirk, smugness, contentment, mirth, deception or honor and courage? On what rational basis can the viewer be sure if this "capturing of the face" is genuine, or on what basis do we ascertain a deception?[8]

Addressing these questions invariably leads to several disconcerting responses. Many of us, consciously or not, have learned to evoke certain facial gestures to mislead those looking at us. The raised eyebrows, a twitch of the nose, the wrinkled forehead can just as easily convey genuine contact or the pretense of understanding. Fans of detective stories find an unpredictable array of faces that convey likely innocence or probable guilt. They are linked to types—the Lothario, femme fatale, spoiled millionaire child, ambitious college grad, bully tycoon, petty thugs, seductive neighbor or lone wolf.

It is common knowledge that fixing and remaking people's faces has become a billion-dollar industry in many countries. While cosmetic surgery originally began as a medical attempt to help World War I soldiers regain some semblance of a normal face after burns and infections from incendiary and chemical weapons, it is now available to anyone who has extra cash to fatten the lips, tuck in some flabby jowls, smooth out wrinkles around the eyes, or blur over aging spots. Not only does the cosmetic surgery business try to keep a face from ever appearing old, it also appeals to one who wants a face that looks more Caucasian, more Oriental, more Mediterranean. Martin Stevens' luminous accounts of deception in nature—among insects, birds, sea creatures—explain the varied tricks in order for survival, food and procreation to be assured. Yet humans remain far more ingenious.[9]

As the preeminent translator and commentator on Emmanuel Levinas, Lingis's discussions of the face are obviously influenced by Levinas's numerous accounts of how the face anchors our ontological and ethical relation to the Other. His writings prepared the directions for Lingis's many studies of encounters, the face-to-face meeting and the anticipating into the unknown. There is a mystical element to face, in Levinas's view. "It is neither seen nor touched—for in visual or tactile sensation the identity of the I envelopes the alterity of the object, which becomes precisely a content."[10] In response to another's face, one understands the taboo of murder and the condemnation of war. The face, to face another, initiates our relation to another's language, truth, belief and value. This relation is more than a personal concern insofar as it also invokes a question or context of our relation to love, death, society and humanity. In the face-to-face encounter one is not apprehending the other but serving the other. In Levinas's words:

> The face in its nakedness as a face presents to me the destitution of the poor one and the stranger; but this poverty and exile which appeal to my powers, address me, do not deliver themselves over to these powers, address me, do not deliver themselves over to these powers as givens, remain the expression of the face. The poor one, the stranger, presents himself as an equal. His equality within this essential poverty consists in referring to the *third party*, thus present at the encounter, whom in the midst of his destitution the Other already serves. He comes to *join* me. But he joins me to himself for service; he commands me as a Master.[11]

Since his translations and first book, Lingis has constantly reworked and rethought these themes on the face as developed by Levinas. He has gradually distanced himself from some of Levinas's central views on the centrality of freedom, a holistic self and God's place in our relation to the Other. He argues that there is a metaphysics of the face in Levinas's writings that presents uncertain implications. First, Levinas's account is committed to a monotheistic god rather than other possible ways of embracing the sacred and divine. Second, there remains a presumption of the negative or lack in an encounter with another that does not respond to the "positive fullness" of another's being. Third, the status and function of the third party is vague and potentially ominous, as the third party could just as easily be an oppressive state rather than a benevolent deity. And fourth, Levinas presents an ethics of the face that leads to an apolitical perspective on a moral treatment of others, as found in Levinas's own comments on the treatment of non-Jews by Israel.[12]

Amid these reservations, a reader approaches with some trepidation a chapter devoted to Prasadchandra. Right away his face stares at us readers. The chapter begins, "A man can be a sign." You return to Prasadchandra's close-up for a possible sign. Beads of jewelry hang from his neck, eyes are glazed over as if glistening delirium or shock. A thin metal rod is pierced through his cheeks. This is a ceremonial sacrifice, though the temptation is to state the more obvious—a ritual torture among primitives. This moment of the sacred is not oriented to a monotheistic commitment, and thus lies beyond the insights found in Levinas's writings.

Lingis immediately proceeds with an account of the significance of sovereignty in a rational life as held by numerous Western thinkers. By establishing the laws of reason, humans have valued themselves according to their recognition and obedience to these laws. The esteemed person is autonomous, self-legislating and self-maintaining. This introductory account is then juxtaposed with a vivid description of Prasadchandra. He is 5 feet and 6 inches tall, weighs 112 pounds and is 17 years old. His skin seems an illustrious mix of black and blue, and he has 2-inch long finger nails, lean abdomen, sleek limbs, much like his Sinhalese ancestors.

In another juxtaposition, Lingis reviews an account of freedom based on the ideas of Kant and Hegel. Ultimately, he locates a spirit of negativity in this account, negative toward nature and the animal traits in the human while overly positive on mutual recognition and philosophy's intertwining human law and death. Lingis's conclusion or possible solution to this problem is not outlined. He instead provides an illustrious portrayal of Prasadchandra's world and all the 17-year-old men who have and will undergo similar rituals. As if writing a personal letter, Lingis observes:

> You went, Prasadchandra, through midnight to the cremation grounds on the Banks of the Ganga. You put your hand in the ashes of pyres and rubbed burnt sandlewood and burnt blood over your young skin...You have watched infants, the syphilitic, the murdered brought here. You have watched the fires climb out of the arms of the dead trees and turn leprous the stomachs and the faces of bankers, soldiers, and priests.[13]

From this graphic missive Lingis immediately turns to central themes in recent Western thought and the chapter's opening line about man as a sign. One prevailing theme focuses on the phallus sign. Respecting and incorporating this sign is a mark of civilization, showing how humans are able to control or redirect their more savage and erotic desires with their own creative efforts to punish and eradicate those unable to embrace this civilizing characteristic.

The piercing ritual is then described. In case of a harsh reaction, men will have to hold the arms and legs of Prasadchandra. The steel skewers are adorned with little pennants and, right after Prasadchandra opens his mouth, the guru Krisnhananda pushes a skewer through his cheeks. No blood appears. The next skewer will go through his tongue. If you are like me, it is impossible to read this description the first time without a shiver or two.

Again, Lingis offers no direct interpretation of either the presentation of mainstream Western ideas or this account of the ritual. He leaves that for the reader. Ending the essay, we realize the juxtapositions are not just another replay of undermining Western reason while celebrating aboriginal culture, or mocking the shortcomings of important thinkers in order to sentimentalize a startling ritual in a non-Western country.

Lingis does not deny the suffering that Bataille would emphasize in this ceremonial piercing. "The caustic density of the pain routs the ego in its retreat. Not a muscle stiffened, nothing was confronted, nothingness was not confronted." In contrast to the Western emphasis on rationality, permanent identity and enduring self, however, Lingis detects in this ritual a more affirmative possibility: The compassion, the impermanence and the no-self.[14]

Individuals

Someone's story is not the same as a chronicle or narrative of one's life. A story of one's life is more than a video transcription of all the things that have occurred. In telling one another our stories, Lingis contends we highlight, replay, forget, embellish and distort the things that have happened in our lives. A chronicle or narrative tends to focus on documented and provable events that have happened.

The significance of stories has been raised by recent humanist or enlightenment versions of pragmatism. Richard Rorty is one of the more prominent figures who believe the sharing of each other's tales brings communities together and enriches their solidarity. Here stories focus on works of fiction that portray the ideals and shortcomings of a society, or they reflect a communicative or discourse ethic in which tellers and listeners appreciate their commonality as well as the differences. Or the communal moment affirms a sense of purpose and their belonging to or yearning for a holistic moment when everything comes together.

This option does not focus on the singularity of the lived stories of others. Lingis contends that this pragmatist approach overlooks the stories we actually tell ourselves and one another. In exchanging stories we tend to present more poetic, dramatic and laughable elements while intermixing disappointments and tragic aspects of our experiences that dwell on the negative and depressing, as if beseeching others to commiserate with our disappointments.

The tales we tell ourselves and others seldom mirror some larger harmony or cultural pattern. In his view, "Yet the story I tell myself about who I am and where is unlike any story ever told. I find that my situation, my vision, the accidents and windfalls on my path do not fit into the available cultural patterns of epic, opera, tragedy, romance, ballet, comedy, vaudeville, sitcom, or farce...Even if I am everyman and no one, I am so in a here and now that has never before occurred and will never be repeated."[15]

The depiction of stories in modern pragmatism is an abstraction. It does not turn its attention to the singular stories behind faces with smiles and grimaces, their toothless grins and decorated head gears, the joyous and sorrowful eyes. Before turning these images into some microcosmic reflection of a general humanity or harmonious society, Lingis first wants to address the meanings and traits of the stories on their own terms as much as possible. Not because they are outside or beyond a cultural pattern, but because, in his words, "These traits fascinate us because on their faces they are each time incomparably individual."[16]

Notes

1. Friedrich Nietzsche, *Human, All Too Human,* trans. R.J. Hollingdale (Cambridge: Cambridge University Press, 1986), #638, "The Wanderer", 203.

2. Alphonso Lingis, *The Imperative* (Bloomington: Indiana University Press, 1998), Ch. 18.

3. Alphonso Lingis, *The Community of Those Who Have Nothing*

in Common (Bloomington: Indiana University Press, 1994), 68.

4. Alphonso Lingis, *Contact* (Lithuania: Baltos Lankos, 2010), 5. In interviews Lingis acknowledges his initial reservations about using a camera. Soon he realized its potential to manifest a sense of reality not quite grasped by the immediate person-to-person encounter. "But the photo image retains its bond with the fragment or event that once became pure presence. We look at the image of our godmother, immigrant from the old country, standing in a field of high grass holding us when we were a six-months old baby, and we are transported back to that field and the warm bosom of that woman long dead." See interview with Bobby George and Tom Sparrow, in *Itinerant Philosophy: On Alphonso Lingis,* editors Bobby George and Tom Sparrow (Brooklyn, NY: Punctum Books, 2014), 14.

5. Marilyn Johnson, *The Dead Beat: Lost Souls, Lucky Stiffs, and the Perverse Pleasures of Obituaries* (New York: Harpers Collins, 2006), 95.

6. Ibid, 97.

7. Alphonso Lingis, *Excesses: Eros and Culture* (Albany: SUNY Press, 1984), 162.

8. Angus Trumble, *A Brief History of the Smile* (New York: Basic Books, 2004).

9. Elizabeth Haiken, *A History of Cosmetic Surgery* (Baltimore: Johns Hopkins University Press, 2000). There are numerous works on cosmetic surgery. What distinguishes Haiken's account is how she first addresses the birth of cosmetic surgery as medical advances to treat deformed faces suffered from severe injuries among World War I soldiers. When wealthy people began inquiring about this technology to conceal the aging process, professions considered such efforts as "vanity medicine." Toward the late 1940s and early 1950s, when psychologists determined that self-esteem was

a medical issue directly related to how one felt about one's looks, cosmetic surgery became more accepted and widely practiced. Bernadette Wegenstein addresses styles of film and the emergence of social media to highlight the recurring fascination with the perfect face. See *The Cosmetic Gaze: Body Modification and the Construction of Beauty* (Cambridge, MA: The MIT Press, 2012). On the immense variety of deceptions in nature, see Martin Stevens, *Cheats and Deceits: How animals and plants exploit and mislead.* (United Kingdom: Oxford University Press, 2016).

10. Emmanuel Levinas, *Totality and Infinity,* trans. Alphonso Lingis (Pittsburgh: Duquesne University Press, 1961), 194.

11. Ibid., 213. For closer analysis of Lingis's philosophical relation to Levinas, see Wolfgang W. Fuchs, "Love and Lust after Levinas and Lingis", Richard I. Sugarman, "The Importance of Alphonso Lingis in Introducing Emmanuel Levinas to America", and Randolph C. Wheeler, "Imperative Innovations", all appearing in *Passion in Philosophy,* ed. Wheeler (Lanham, MD: Lexington Books, 2017). For Lingis's critical approaches to Levinas, see his "Three Objections to Levinas' Philosophy", *Graduate Faculty Philosophy Journal* 30 (2009), and "Six Problems in Levinas's Philosophy", *PhaenEx: Journal of Existential and Phenomenological Theory and Culture* 7 (2012).

12. Alphonso Lingis, "The Metaphysics of the Face", *Philosophy Today* (Winter, 2013).

13. Lingis, *Excesses,* 122.

14. Ibid., 131.

15. Alphonso Lingis, *The First Person Singular* (Evanston, ILL: Northwestern University Press, 2007), 54.

16. Alphonso Lingis, *Body Transformations* (New York: Routledge, 2005), 7.

Chapter Two

Nomad Ethos

*Open space unrestricted by walls, either at the seashore or on a
mountainside, liberated the human imagination. The conviviality
afforded confabulators the chance to shine, to engage in spontaneous
tournaments during which those who recounted the most beguiling
tale, retold the most extraordinary events, would reap regard. Facts
mixed here with fancy, times and places were misstated, legends
were born, myths arose.*
Ryszard Kapuscinski[1]

Being at Home

Neuroanthropologist John Allen has studied numerous features
that have emerged among *homo sapiens* while adjusting to and
embracing life within a stable and lasting habitat. Language,
sympathy, symbolic meanings, security, exceptionally increased
longevity and control of environment are among the many traits
that have separated the modern human from other primates.
These traits, or genetic advantages as evolutionists call them, are
centered upon the human ability to establish permanent abodes
or dwellings that offer a haven from the more dangerous and
reckless features of external realities. As Allen notes, "Home
is a place where we can balance out lives with the imbalance
imposed by the outside world."[2]

The home is more than just a physical structure. It evokes
an attitude or feeling that underscores a sense of belonging.
This belonging has considerable range, from establishing a
distinct nursery room for an infant's early days to building a
neighborhood near a cemetery in which burial spaces of the
deceased should remain within proximity. Neuroantropologists
note that humans, despite their various tastes for dwellings, are

not necessarily the most efficient builders. The nests of insects and birds tend to be much more reliable than human shanties and trailer parks. We are ambivalent, never sure when or where to build tents, shacks, palaces, hovels or McMansions. Mammals and primates tend to find their home directly within the natural surroundings, digging burrows in the desert or rearranging leaves and twigs to make a sleeping pad in the bottom of a tree trunk. The closest contact many humans have with nature during sleep is by nestling their heads in down-filled pillows.

Investigating the artifacts and bones of our proto-human ancestors, researchers postulate that the hunter-gatherer clearly gave way to what seems to be a genetic mutation insofar as the modern human continually seeks more secure, better equipped, often larger homes, even if only one or two persons are residing in it.

This search is central to the emergence of *homo economicus* (the rational animal that weighs long and short-term gains/losses). The relative wealth that comes in owning a home in comfortable surroundings and neighborhoods provides confidence, leisure time, opportunities to experiment more with art, food or entertainment, and tranquil moments for reflection or personal interests.

Home dwelling provides additional opportunities to tell and hear stories. According to Allen, the circulation of stories is integral to *homo sapiens'* penchant for home—the ability to use language. It provides an essential resource in terms of local and distant communication and coordinating a sense of community of home dwellers with their neighbors and fellow citizens. We deploy linguistic skills by exchanging narratives in order to appreciate one another's place in the world. When positive stories abound, they act as a sort of contagion that can lead to "epidemics of confidence."[3] By contrast, negative stories as those exchanged among or about the homeless deflate confidence and immobilize rather than energize our life's options. When catching news reports about abandoned children, desperate refugees, the insane wandering the streets aimlessly, Allen believes we become convinced of the correlation between home and a more humane life.

Lingis's writings present a rejoinder to this valorization of the domestic life by arguing that the nomadic ethos remains an enduring and essential trait of humanity. This ethos can be found in three themes. One, the trust placed in a stranger captures an exhilarating human moment. Two, the nomadic ethos embodies the vagaries of accompaniment, such as being with those going through misfortune and those facing their own death. Three, the prevalence of sacred locales and holy temples welcoming pilgrims and aliens illuminates a humaneness that one infrequently finds in private homes, walled-in neighborhoods or gated communities.

Trusting Strangers

For the past two generations children have been regularly warned about strangers. Milk cartons featuring a photo of an abducted child, posters and television programs highlighting a "Have You Seen Me?" message of a lost teenager, and routine reminders in schools that students should beware of strangers both in the hallways as well as on their way home. Admittedly fearing a stranger or leaving the familiar path occasionally appears in classic tales, as seen in "Little Red Riding Hood." Today's reminders about the stranger are much more pervasive, given 24/7 access to news via social media. Indeed, one may liken today's manufactured fears of strangers to those growing up in the Cold War generation when school children regularly prepared for air raids by huddling under their desks and folding over their bodies in the hallways.

Such efforts about suspicious strangers have had negligible results in terms of improved social policy or moral pedagogy. For example, milk cartons no longer feature children's faces because it is now common knowledge that a youngster is most likely to be abducted by one with a familiar rather than unfamiliar face. The most prevalent cases of child sexual abuse continue to be found among readily recognized faces—those of neighbors, teachers, priests, coaches. Tagging offenders as "sexual predators" has had no appreciable effect on the actual or prospective rates of sexual offenses. In the language of criminologists, these efforts have not made any demonstrable reduction in the fears and actual crime rates of specific violations. To the contrary, as the definition of "sexual abuse or assault" continues to expand, whether on college campuses or in the military, some claim there is an epidemic or culture of sexual violation.

These public actions, regardless of their uneven accomplishments, have hindered and deflated the nomadic impulse that brings about some of our most treasured or haunting experiences. This impulse arises when trusting someone we have never met and, rather than caution and fear, the moment entices intense, joyous, erotic, pedagogical and aesthetic senses. Lingis presents an array of descriptions of such moments, sparked or sustained by the stories exchanged and enlivened. Each telling and retelling raises questions about our own conventional views and philosophical givens.

"The act of trust is a leap into the unknown," Lingis asserts in an essay titled "Typhoons". The essay has nothing to do with actual typhoons, other than a brief reference to chaos theory's speculation that massive storms in North America could be sparked by the slightest disturbance upon air movements by butterfly wings in the South America winds. It begins with details about the history, political debacles and environment of Madagascar. The author is invited by a friend to have a guide lead them through the country's dense jungle. Unlike the author, wearing the wrong clothes and unprepared for the terrain, the guide Javalson is in his element, walking easily in the wild brush and unmarked paths.

Then it dawns upon Lingis that Javalson is quite capable of stealing his camera, backpack, funds, even taking his life—without getting caught. As they return to the village, Lingis asks someone who speaks French to tell him about the guide. A translator relays that Javalson said some things about himself and his people, but mostly joked and laughed with the villagers about this American traveler who had absurd notions about dressing for the jungle. After a brief exchange of gifts, Javalson departs into the unknown.

Abruptly, the reader is taken to London where on a pleasant evening a bomb explodes in a crowded street. Several days later there is another bombing in a district of immigrants. What follows is the now so familiar: widespread panic, non-stop media coverage, hundreds of casualties, many fatal, then the usual parade of experts appearing before citizens to explain the carnage. Lingis offers little commentary.

He instead abruptly returns to Madagascar, one of the ten poorest countries in the world, to remind the reader that Javalson is a "local man encountered by chance on the path" with whom he feels completely secure. Then the reader is back again to wealthy and western London, one of the centers of modern democracy and progress, where one senses only "pervasive fear."[4] Lingis describes how trust in the unknown and fear of the unknown share the same source, yet are pulling or pushing us in contrary directions. In the London bombings, the culprit was not a crazed foreigner but a 23-year-old engineering student who had an apartment in the neighborhood. Many local acquaintances knew him as a decent but quiet person.

Within the secrecy of his home where he built the bombs the young engineering student ruined lives of fellow residents. By contrast, the openness of the jungle shows a guide making sure the strange American traveler enjoys his trek as much as possible. Which option conveys a more convincing account of our potential humaneness?

This potential also appears in a completely different climate—the steppes of Mongolia. The essay titled "Space Travel" initially conjures images of leaving Earth's hemisphere into outer space. The title winds up referring to the many overwhelming spaces traversed by the nomads in Mongolia. They are described as luminous, practical, made for working, hunting and shepherding. Their knowledge of the steppes is so intricate that they can identify and live by innumerable plant and animal species distinct only to Mongolia.

In these vast and startling spaces nomads are rarely alone. As they return from their daily tasks, the night is filled with stories about oddities and moments of the day. Lingis acknowledges he does not know their language, but watching them laugh and clap and getting notes from a translator, he conveys to the reader the fascinating details of the nomads' recalling near accidents, sightings of or threats from animals, forbidding weather, ancestral traditions and sundry events. In Lingis's words, "The nomad camp is the arena of circulation of people, where every event becomes a story that surprises and entertains, where places and events from long ago and far away are held in narratives retold and shared." [5]

Conference attendees and skeptics often contend that Lingis does not actually present any arguments. In place of more conventional uses of premises and conclusions, they see Lingis providing elaborate and stylistic descriptions that switch focal points and contexts, but without offering a series of claims in some logical structure. More than one observer has surmised that Lingis is more of a lyrical poet than a philosopher.

This charge is not entirely accurate. In his reflections about nomadic life Lingis actually does present a clear-cut argument. First, we consider two options for realizing human potential. One position is that the physical and emotional sense of home makes us human. A second position is that the nomadic impulse is central to our humanity. There is widespread evidence for the first position, as found in recent research of neuroanthropologists, evolutionists and social psychologists. Its position looks at the nomadic impulse as outdated, impractical and a sentimental vestige of distant ancestors. Recounting his jungle trek in Madagascar, related travels and other researchers on human mobility, Lingis provides considerable support for the enduring significance of nomadic urges.

This juxtaposition winds up being a disjunctive syllogism. A or B. Not B. Therefore A. Advocates of the domestic life opt for A (the home makes us human) over B (the nomadic life, and to be negated) as the most defining facet of modern humanity. For Lingis, there is no inherent conflict between home life and nomadic life. He clearly does not reject A. In his words, "The home base is a pole of repose and departure. The zone of the intimate is a pole of warmth and tranquility that we keep sight of as we advance into the stretches of the alien and that our nomadic wanderings gravitate back to."[6] Contrary to neuroanthropologists, Lingis sees the home and the nomad as compatible or complementary modes of human life.

What poses the greater threat to Lingis's approach to this syllogism is a third disjunct—technopoles.[7] These are growing if not unstoppable movements of modern civilization that quash the nomadic impulses. Their centers—New York, Hong Kong, Sao Paola, Moscow, Beijing, Singapore, Silicon Valley, London, Berlin, among many others—are rooted in a mix of rather disparate political and cultural backgrounds. What they have in common is the drive and desire to extend their powers through the continual expansion of their borders, not just in terms of physical lines of separation, but in the capacity to keep a panoptic eye on all those who live within and outside them.

The estimated one billion people who comprise these various technopoles consign the rest of the world's population to an outer zone, as the technopoles dictate the modes of contact through airports, movement of basic foods, development and ownership of sophisticated weapons, railroads and now social media. Central to their powers is the inventive use of instruments and computers to measure the movements and unfamiliar figures that elude their scope and institutions. Technopoles are ravenous in their appetites. They desire and need constant energy, more land and weakened threats to their mini-empires to ensure their health and growth.

With this disjunctive syllogism, Lingis finds that the home or nomad option is not a problem. The threat to the nomadic ethos arises in the emergence of a third disjunct—technopoles, which sees domestic life as one mode for consolidating and expanding the evolution of technopoles. They do not condone the freedom nor appreciate the independence that marked the earliest humans who never stayed in one place. The antithesis for technopoles is the nomadic ethos.

In Accompaniment

Years ago a student was completing her Bachelor's Degree, over a decade since she obtained her Associates Degree and began a career as a full-time nurse. On occasion she told the class about some of her experiences with sickly and elderly patients. Some would recover and go home while others knew they would never see home again. The student had a comforting and quirky sense of humor that became quite a virtue when attending to patients. Abiding by the axiom that sometimes humor really is the best medicine, she cautioned that when to laugh with a patient is a delicate issue. Obviously she does not want to make light of the patient's medical conditions. Nor does she want to try to tell jokes as a way of getting the patient to force a smile.

The student encouraged future nurses, and any of us who eventually accompany others in their despair and suffering, to improvise by first encouraging the patient to talk about his or her life. Listening to patients one gets a sense of their attitudes toward the immediate medical prognosis and their sense of humor. With a nurse's patience, says the student, patients will soon be delighted to tell some stories of their lives—memorable, trivial, absurd or simply amusing. Before you know it, the student notes, you begin relaying snippets and anecdotes from your own stories to the patient. As the nurse is often quite younger, the patient becomes curious about her life, possible friends and lovers, vacations or future adventures. You know you have struck a chord, she tells the class, when the patient wants to know when you will return on your next shift.

One very old and sickly woman took a quick turn for the worse and knew she would be unlikely to survive the night. Her son got word and immediately went to catch a plane and be with her by early afternoon. Unfortunately, there was a November snowstorm in Minneapolis and the son's flight departure was delayed until late evening. Afraid she would die before the arrival of her son, the patient asked the nurse if she could stay past her shift. Perhaps she could read some poems and Old Testament passages, or sing some Jewish songs.

The nurse chuckled, admitting that she is not Jewish and cannot carry a tune. This brought a smile to the patient, noting it did not matter, as long as the nurse could tell stories or hum any tunes long enough until her son arrived. The nurse did and held her hand. The patient died an hour after her son finally made it to the hospital room.

A nomad ethos thrives not only in exotic lands and foreign travels. The recognition and solace offered to a stranger, particularly one suffering and dying, can arise in the most ordinary circumstances. Such moments and traditions of providing solace are the beginnings of mortal communities. They are central to many of Lingis's writings, such as when he observes: "But beneath and prior to this, we make contact and establish community with the other in the touch that caresses his or her carnal surfaces and that is afflicted with, obsessed by, their vulnerability, susceptibility, mortality—the touch that has no power to and does not seek to heal, but has to go accompany the other in her or her own dying."[8]

The most theoretical support of this observation is found in *Deathbound Subjectivity*. Lingis introduces this book by addressing the varied attacks on human subjectivity. Heidegger, postmodern writers, the emergence of physics and Darwinism pose considerable challenges to the human subject—a figure who needs to have self-understanding, a sense of mortality, a feeling of freedom, in order to have a meaningful life, personally and socially. While this human subject has numerous similarities with other primates and other species, its relation to death seems quite distinct.

This relation is reexamined throughout the book. Chapter One, "The Origin of Infinity", presents a philosophical exchange between Husserl and Nietzsche on the relations of death, finitude, science and responsibility. Lingis retraces the thinking behind each position, particularly the one that emphasizes the natural in the human in contrast to the human that dictates to nature. At stake is a true, identifiable or genuine humanity. According to Lingis, "The pursuit of Western science and practice eventually transforms nature, to be sure, but first it transforms human nature." [9]

One expression of this transformation is found in the *Deathbound Subjectivity*'s being punctuated with passages from section #337, "A humaneness of the future," in Nietzsche's *The Gay Science*. Most of the attention on the traditions of *ars moriendi*, different cultures on treating the dying, or rituals respecting the corpse, focus on what we have lost or are about to lose and the battle over the soul's destiny that will soon confront the deceased. Lingis focuses on a particular human component among those who accompany others that is joyous or affirming. He extends the closing passage from Nietzsche about the poorest sailor rowing with golden oars to another kind of humaneness: one who accompanies another in his or her final moments.[10]

31

This humaneness departs from the humanisms presented in existentialism, Marxism, Christianity or modern psychology. For these outlooks humans are primarily individuals with a core self. Being estranged from this self continues to be one of the central themes in analyses and treatments of individuals who have lost themselves to drug addiction, a mental disorder or disease of aging and memory loss. The related questions about freedom, responsibility and anxiety invariably see accompanying others as an inability to provide solace or reconciliation at the right moment.

One sense of Lingis's proposal for another kind of humaneness emphasizes a freedom from the self, specifically the on-going concerns with self-consciousness, deliberating one's motives and the impressions our actions have on others, weighing out positives and negatives. These concerns can be debilitating when faced with another's suffering.

Before closing with a final reflection on Nietzsche, Lingis ends *Deathbound Subjectivity* with reflections on those in accompaniment. There is no rational purpose to their task, "save to render present the serving of the other unto the abysses of his or her dying, in order that the other be not lost into solitude, into the night and fog." Furthermore, this task has an unexpected result. For a sentence later Lingis highlights the affirmative aspect of accompaniment, "It is not an act that *I* do; it is the passion which dispossesses me of my own citadel of selfhood..."[11]

In sum, there is considerable evidence supporting Lingis's contention that nomadic life—be it worldly travels or accompanying those who are suffering—remains a central human trait that is undervalued in the domestic thesis and threatened with extinction in a world overwhelmed by technopoles. While zoologists and hikers into the wild have observed cases of animals assisting other creatures in a mortal moment, none of them have drawn the sustained interest that has been devoted to humans accompanying others facing their final hours. In the writings of Lingis, one finds this ethos in nearly every human culture's ancient traditions and common practices.

Temples and The Sacred

Georges Bataille approached the sacred through its various depictions of some of the most cruel and sadistic rituals of humanity. From religious ceremonies to political spectacles, Bataille detects a fascination humans have when it comes to observing or inflicting horrible pains upon other members of their own species. His starkly illustrated *Tears of Eros* recounts how severe suffering can be portrayed or explained through the lens of justice, redemption and salvation. Much of this evidence appears in paintings, statues and architecture. Bataille then presents photographs of an early twentieth century execution torture in China sent from an acquaintance.[12] The reader comes upon a condemned man given opium so that he can stay conscious—and even grin—while his legs and arms are sawed off. Each photo shows a gradual withdrawal from life, albeit the spectators seem ever more entranced by the unfolding horror.

Sacrifice derives from making separate. In Bataille's terms, the sacred is a break from the everyday world to a spiritual or divine world. Animals do not undergo this transition, as "every animal is *in the world like water in water.*" To the contrary, humans invariably establish an occasional distance or reversal of this world as if the sacred world offers a respite from a daily life of labor, materialism and utility. "Elements of this situation can be grasped by human intelligence, but the animal cannot *realize* them."[13]

Bataille's point should not be construed as admittance of the superiority of the human. The sacred promises to be a blessing but is more often a curse for humans. While the earthly order of things presents the individual as content, anguished and lost, Bataille sees the sacred as offering a renewed intimacy with the divine order of things. This yearning condemns humans to paradoxical options, including celebratory festivals, communal orgies and rituals to contagions of danger and world wars.[14]

Lingis, much influenced by Bataille's thoughts on excess, presents a more affirmative and earthly account of the sacred. This is particularly evident in his perspective on temples and religious sites. Second to the photographs of human faces, pictures of sacred places and holy temples draw the most frequent appearances in Lingis's published works. *Excesses* features the erotic temple in "Khajuraho." Two early photographs in *Dangerous Emotions* are of the statues in Easter Island and the grinning Buddha. "The Art of War", chapter 21 in *Violence and Splendor*, begins with a stone-etched portrayal of a man gleefully ready to take his sword and behead the fearful victim. A closing chapter in *Foreign Bodies* situates a modern high rise next to an ancient cemetery. *Trust* presents a photo of the imposing artifice Petra, a temple carved into a huge cliff. It introduces Lingis's meditations on the various experiences an unsuspecting traveler might have when suddenly facing this temple which lacks any utilitarian functions. Another chapter describes a series of small churches in the remote mountains of Ethiopia. "Good Deeds", the concluding chapter of *Body Transformations*, opens with a stark and stunning portrait of a man entering the Grand Mosque in Mali.

According to Thomas Altizer, there is a sacred element in most voyages. In Lingis's voyages Altizer recognizes an ambivalence of a Catholic education, the turmoil of pronouncements on laws against lust amid the erotic transgressions of the most solemn declarations on the ascetic ideal, and the simple desires of the profane world over the unclear promises of the divine world. Is there a universal eucharist, asks Altizer? He finds a possible answer in Lingis. "If nothing else, Lingis's work demonstrates that we have truly forgotten a universal eucharist, and therefore have forgotten sacrifice itself, or the depths of sacrifice."[15]

Gilles Deleuze sees Nietzsche as initiating a philosophical

inquiry into the risks and discoveries of a wandering mind. Academic thought tends to nurturing and sustaining familiar controversies and debates, reflecting the principals and codes of society: law, contracts and institutions. Deleuze finds Nietzsche embodying a nomad ethos that defies or mocks these codes. The movement driven by this ethos can be geographic mobility as well as levels of intensity. In 1973 Deleuze asked, "Who are our nomads today, our real Nietzscheans?"[16]

A Stranger Welcomed

One possible answer is found in the work of Lingis. He presents a two-fold account of the relation of nomad life and the sacred. First, the depths of sacrifice often bear no universal dimension and the nomadic impulse is not driven by the Socratic dictum of "Know Thyself" or the quest for realizing a component of human nature. Second, Lingis discovers the sacred interwoven with the nomad ethos in a relatively simple encounter: welcoming the stranger.

Humans build and maintain temples in specific locales to which anyone can visit and feel at home. Here the sacred is more than violence, painful rituals and ceremonial cremations. The temple, as its etymology indicates — "cut off", implies a separate space from the everyday. Lingis does not pursue Bataille's investigation of the human paradox of seeking a return to the divine world of intimacy. He instead takes Bataille's notion of excess as a way of conveying to the reader the generosity and welcoming powers of temples and those who tender them.

Lingis's portrayal of Lalibela is a memorable example.[17] There is first simply the arduous effort to reach these 13 churches carved out of the Ethiopian mountains. Before a road was built, it took 8 days on mule; with a sturdy jeep it is now a 2-day venture. To visit these temples still requires plenty of walking and climbing, up steep hills and through tunnels and rock crevices. Peering through a passageway, one might spot a priest or hermit quietly reading or praying.

According to scholars, there is no complete and satisfactory explanation for the existence of these churches. Why out of rock, so they will be more permanent than human built churches? Why so remote, as a test of the depth of a believer's faith? Or were these churches the center of a vibrant society that has long been extinguished?

Lingis too can only speculate. He acknowledges that to imagine these churches being constructed today is impossible. He admits it is difficult to sort out the historical movements and political struggles surrounding these temples. He attests that to finally arrive at this sacred place one realizes an orgy of sensations. He or she will be seeing like an eagle, hearing a silence and stillness that is intoxicating, feeling the strength and age of the rocks and carvings. And most of all, like a pilgrim who seeks Lalibela, the stranger who by chance meets one of the hermits dwelling among the churches will be greeted like a brother or sister.

Notes

1. Ryszard Kapuscinski, *Travels with Herodotus,* trans. Klara Glowczewska (New York: Knopf, 2007), 178.
2. John S. Allen, *Home: How Habitat Made Us Human* (New York: Basic/Perseus, 2015), 31.
3. Ibid., *152.*
4. Alphonso Lingis, *Trust* (Minneapolis: University of Minnesota Press, 2004), 65. The inverse relation between fear and trust, as well as political forces that distort the potential of crime and fear of the criminal, is documented in a range of political perspectives. See the libertarian magazine *Reason*'s issue on "Why is the FBI so Obsessed with Sex?" 48/11 (April 2017) and liberal scholarly approach in Jean Comaroff and John L. Comaroff's *The Truth About Crime:*

Sovereignty Knowledge, Social Order (Chicago: The University of Chicago Press, 2016). For an interdisciplinary and public policy approach, see essays and articles appearing in the special edition of *The Long Term View* (7/2, Winter 2010), "The Incarceration Society."

5. Alphonso Lingis, *Violence and Splendor* (Evanston, Ill: Northwestern University Press, 2011), 16.

6. Lingis, *The Imperative,* 42.

7. Alphonso Lingis, "Death Drive" *Journal of Value Inquiry* 29 (1995), 220-224. Also see, "In Orbit" *Journal of Social Philosophy* 25/3 (Winter, 1994), and "Anger", in *On Jean-Luc Nancy,* ed. Darren Sheppard, Simon Sparks, and Colin Thomas (London: Routledge, 1997), where Lingis notes that technopoles emphasize computer savvy intelligence, control of transportation systems, and an archipelago of surveillance techniques. "The inhabitants of the urban technopoles are not engaged in industrial production. They are engaged in the programming and management of industry and commerce." (200).

8. Alphonso Lingis, *Foreign Bodies* (New York: Routledge, 1994), 185.

9. Alphonso Lingis, *Deathbound Subjectivity* (Bloomington, IN: University of Indiana Press, 1989), 20, 36.

10. Ibid., 77.

11. Ibid., 190.

12. Georges Bataille, *Tears of Eros* (San Francisco: City Lights Press, 1988).

13. Georges Bataille, *Theory of Religion,* Trans. Robert Hurley (New York: Zone Books, 1992), 19.

14. Ibid., Ch. 3.

15. Thomas J. Altizer, "The Sacred Vision of a Solitary Voyager", and see David Farrell Krell, "Far From the Pallid Float", in *Encounters With Alphonso Lingis,* ed. Alexander E. Hooke and Wolfgang Fuchs (Lanham Md.: Lexington Books), 48.

16. Gilles Deleuze, "Active and Reactive", in *The New Nietzsche,* ed. David Allison (New York: Dell Publishing), 1977.

17. Lingis, *Trust,* 164.

Chapter Three

We as Collage - Not a Collective

For Walt Fuchs

We Without Apology

Lingis is unabashed in his uses of we. He does not speak about a privileged we, an exemplary or hegemonic we, or "we." According to him, the various ways critics qualify their references to first person plural (we, us, our) are unnecessary, if not unjustifiable. Their caution and skepticism about any direct use of we invariably lead one to focus on this important pronoun as if it were a rhetorical sleight of hand, an ironic twist, a sign of embarrassment or elitism.

Worse, their gradual cynicism diminishes or derides the reality of those whose contact with others can only be articulated in terms of we or our. Thus readers, and students subject to these theoretical reservations, are tempted to circumvent any substantive meaning to first person plural in their own reflections and research. Given the persuasive charms of these reservations, to admit a genuine or lived we involves the risk of being charged with superficiality, a lack of sophistication, nostalgia or political naiveté.[1]

In the face of this risk, Lingis writes in first person plural without apology. Seemingly oblivious to the on-going controversies over any legitimate use of *we*—as if it connotes self-indulgence of self-delusion, Lingis depicts experiences and contacts that embody a substance to first person plural. These contacts are presented directly and with little hesitation, as they often move one to awaken to daring, brazen or unfamiliar individuals in their contexts and surroundings. To present them requires an air of innocence to the extent that the contacts appear as new to the writer as they are to the reader. They encompass more than surprise and spectacle. They also initiate beliefs and emotions that embrace other truths: unfamiliar expressions of gods, strange forms of human commitments, eccentric relations humans have with the past and future, but also with animals, trees and unseen spirits. These truths evoke the kinds of genuine goods and values that are better conceived not as potential instantiations or counterexamples to our generalizations and conventions, but rather as compelling additions to our own senses of reality and truth.

In writing about *we* or *us*, however, Lingis also raises some critical stakes. While conversant with most of the influential figures and themes discussed under the postmodern rubric, he extends their central ideas to new levels and fields of inquiry.

Instead of scrutinizing the uses of first person plural or maintaining a respectable distance from them, his philosophical endeavors are distinct insofar as they address: how do we, he and his audience respond to the many kinds of contact that are readily dismissed insofar as they are overlooked in our scholarly and philosophical endeavors? What might these other uses and realities of the first person plural say that affirm, question or contest us? Can his own writings contribute to contemporary discussions about the possibilities and pitfalls of human relations, cultural and political entities, social and biological communities and the theoretical or critical reflections on them?

Collage

Lingis's answers are guided by looking at *we* more as a collage and less as a collective. A collage, unlike a collection, emphasizes or highlights the unpredictable ways that humans and other life forms come together. The use of *we* as a collective—whether the result of unconscious drives, chosen ideologies, an intersubjective ethic or rational communication acts—emphasizes certain values, particularly those that help us to distinguish whether the experiences of we can be understood or appreciated in terms of true or false, good or bad, genuine or superficial, beautiful or ugly, familiar and significant terms for making judgments about moral, social and biological forms. Such judgments are derived from a reflective pose, calling for public verification, scholarly erudition or rational and deliberative dialog.

Although he does on occasion speak of collective events, such as those spawned by gifts[2], Lingis is reluctant to attribute any overarching perspective to them in the name of a social order or political model. A home, for example, is more than an anchor for family life, it is also a point of departure; familiar landscapes and harmonious environs are also places of separation and disconnection.[3]

A collage, by contrast, suspends value judgments made from the perspective of deliberative and purposeful reflection in favor of more primordial ones. Suppose, with Lingis, we first formulate our judgments guided by joy, the sacred, sorrow and laughter? Do these elemental passions not also bring humans together? Indeed, are they not equally compelling? The perspective of a collective begins to address these questions from the assumption of shared truths weighed as valid, unifying or credible. The *we* found in a collage, however, unveils powers that undermine these assumptions by evoking if not celebrating the truths of other realities.

Why collage? According to Harold Rosenberg, the use of collage marked a radical change in modern art by taking disparate images and signs to highlight the ambiguities of life and our understanding of it. Although collage has been a craft wherever and whenever there has been human ingenuity—from flower arrangements and quilts to cooks making something out of leftovers and children sticking scraps together—Rosenberg points out how in the hands of artists collage takes on a revolutionary task of bringing together disparate realities and fragments of identity. "Collage manifests itself," he adds, "in modern art modes as a kind of adversary within the mode itself."[4]

Lingis gives a distinct philosophical twist to collage by inaugurating another kind of adversarial relation to contemporary thought. Interweaving ideas of prominent philosophers and contemporary scholars with colorful accounts of events and figures in strange settings, his essays frequently present juxtapositions of images and gaps, theories and descriptions that echo the patchwork featured in collage art.

Yet we should not be misled. Just as in collage art there are indicators of unity, multiplicity, purpose and farce, so too in many of Lingis's writings there is a logic or structure—blending his style, scholarship, wit and drama—indicating that the presentation of views and insights is not entirely derived by mischief or happenstance. The writings ask the audience to read with both a seriousness and humor in order to inquire into new philosophical insights. At the same time, he warns, much of our confusion begins when misunderstanding or misusing the values of these insights.

He says as much in *Foreign Bodies*. It starts with a sketch of how any population's history, economy, sexuality and national identity are marvelous in their many forms of patchwork. "Our own culture," he later observes, "is a collage of elements retained from the past or evolving more slowly, elements answering to our present ecological, demographic, political, and economic situation, and elements borrowed from other cultures."[5]

The Imperative begins by talking about our cultures—whose languages, homes, commitments or intellectual tasks are likely shared by the reader and the author. Then four of the next five chapters introduce first person plural in their opening sentences. We awaken to the elements, we approach levels of sensual experience, we watch tropical parades, we meet a face and we enjoy our home.

In the Preface Lingis cautions the reader from deriving a unifying theme among sundry imperatives. "Resisting all forms of holism," he notes, "(this book) holds that directives we find in the night, the elements, the home, the alien spaces, the carpentry of things, the halos and reflections of things, the faces of fellow humans, and death have to be described separately."[6]

The subsequent chapters then raise questions about our own belief in self-respect, our imperatives and our sense of human dignity. This solicitation by first person plural sets the pace for Lingis's accounts of disparate realities, strange passions, sacred moments and phantom equators that direct or compel so much of one another's thought and conduct. Throughout this panorama there remains the reflection over things that we *have* to do, people we *need* to attend to and imperatives we *must* act from.

Foreign Bodies — a book with chapter titles about alien feelings and strange lusts that are also our own —starts with a couple of lessons from our ancestors. Citing Nietzsche's insight on the human tendency to celebrate specific corporeal types, Lingis reviews several body ideals introduced among the great cultures or civilizations. Ancient Egypt, with its expertise on the stars and architecture, the Byzantines, high among the grand spiritualists, or Socratic-Euclidean rationality, an anchor for devoted truth seekers, are among the many systems of thought that also envisioned distinct body ideals. In light of this remarkable smorgasbord of body ideals, Lingis invites the reader to consider still new or emerging ideals. Hence he writes about the wish to elucidate not only the theoretical background and implications of the topic, but also, with the help of other sources such as biography, anthropology or literature, visions of "the bodies we might become."[7]

What follows are sketches and stories of sundry figures including beggars, wayward children, weight lifters, Mishima's seppuku, the corpses of peasants, lovers in asylums, guerillas in darkness, fictional creatures found in Michel Tournier or Marguerite Dumas, or human portraits uncovered by Gilbert

Herdt or Diane Ackerman. These sketches form collages that are more than jumbled portraits of body ideals—they are arrangements that also feature ideals in emotions and thoughts. In a word, they are collages of lived possibilities.

Some of these stories and the possibilities they evoke are more elaborately presented in *Abuses* and *Dangerous Emotions*. Calling them philosophy texts is a bit of a stretch, so overtly do they bring in other disciplines while circumventing standard citations of the recent literature in the author's professed field. Indeed, the jacket covers receive the endorsements of anthropologist Michael Taussig and social and literary critic Elizabeth Grosz. In the spirit of the collage—mixing up the earnest, eccentric, unpredictable and ludicrous elements—the individual chapters of these books are a disparate lot. The introductory photos and titles have little in common with one another, as if the chapters were randomly strung together. Yet each presents an adversarial discussion with philosophy and contemporary thought. When critics and scholars discuss gender, empowerment and fairness, for example, Lingis counters by articulating still different kinds of bodies, new forms of sovereignty, and deeds of justice that were driven by love or courage rather than a sense of prudence or fairness.

The photos introducing each chapter illuminate some directions. Frequently they are followed by immediate uses of first person plural. One chapter, "A Doctor in Havana", discusses two women tortured in South America. Lingis begins with several senses in which "what we call speech that is serious claims to speak the truth."[8] Speech, he notes, can be confession, making claims, a response to others, even the circulation of a discourse. There is also a speech that tries to speak for the silenced. This speech contains or offers important truths and enticing realities that give us pause. In this pause Lingis disrupts his lecture (still another kind of speech) by devoting the second half of the essay to an extended quote from Robert Cohen's report, appearing in a covert action bulletin, about a Cuban doctor treating two women tortured by military thugs in Brazil. After depicting the new faces the torturers had left them (for example by surgically inserting dog teeth into their mouths), the report concludes with the women making promises and commitments—still other kinds of speech—to continue the cause. The extended passage, without comment from Lingis, pushes readers to reexamine their speech, and to what extent they or he have the terms to adequately address the report.

The chapter "Violations" introduces phenomena that draw corporeal and spiritual possibilities found in a range of laughing, saddening, contentious and intense passions. With lengthy indented passages highlighting the essay, it can be likened to watching the author holding an adversarial relation with himself. Has he not at one time or another—whether as, say, teacher, writer or respected member of an academic circle—held or endorsed several contrary passions and their related beliefs or ideas? Lingis speculates that most of us do. Yet his reasons are distinctive. They do not bring us nearer to who we are, but they help us see through or past ourselves. The essay then presents how extreme emotions involve joy and grief, laughter and tears not because they affirm a personal identity or bring attention to ourselves, but because they render us transparent. Communication or speech is more than individuals mutually recognizing one another's core self and key interests; the ideals of reciprocity and mutual respect are only infrequent benchmarks of genuine contact. More significantly, Lingis proposes, there is also a communication in which concern for one's own interests are bypassed, thus one can be drawn to prostitutes, gravediggers, hustlers, ascetics and sundry other strange figures.[9]

There is also a paradoxical sense of *we*, as approached in *The Community of Those With Nothing in Common*. With thinkers such as Bataille, Blanchot, Nancy and Nietzsche in the background, Lingis investigates a variety of efforts to establish community in terms of rational discourse, intense passions or shared grief and suffering. Though sympathetic to his predecessors' fascination with the notion of a community that can be thought but not embodied or realized, Lingis finds dramatic moments of community when strangers recognize a sense of kinship to the extent that they give something of themselves to one another. This is manifest in the elements—blood, tears, flesh, but also in moments of consolation, grief and death, when we recognize what is lost, absent or departing. Here, intensity rather than duration is the benchmark for establishing a *we* or *us*. For as soon as the two or more individuals come together in these circumstances and begin to have a sense of what is transpiring, the bond is already dissipating.

Hence, writes Lingis:

> To catch sight, beyond kinship, of this *community in death...* We should have to find ourselves, or put ourselves through imagination, in a situation at the farthest limits from kinship— in a situation in which one finds oneself in a country with which one's own is at war, among foreigners bound in a religion, that one cannot believe or which excludes one, with whom one is engaged in no kind of productive or commercial dealings, who owe one nothing, who do not understand a word of one's language, who are far from one in age...—and on whom one finds oneself completely dependent, for one's very life.[10]

We Who Are on the Same Page

Similar to the editorial *we* used by journalists, Lingis acknowledges there is a genuine relation between the author and his audience. He does not go so far as to invoke the Victorian attitude of concealing first person singular out of humility or prudishness. The intimacies and indulgences in many of his passages are expressed through a mix of references to you, I, he and she. At times these expressions culminate in a *we*, but one that thrives on an ambiguous referent. Frequently the pronouns refer to individuals described or remembered from various stories, encounters and studies that also convey moments when these individuals form a commonality and plurality. Associations, lovers, collaborators, blood brothers, interlocutors, accomplices, are among the many contacts Lingis elucidates. But the contact between author and reader, established solely on a silent page, presents a different dynamic.

On the one hand, Lingis likens the reader to a friend. Many essays, he notes, began as letters to friends. On the other hand, these letters originated in circumstances quite remote from the recipients of these letters, and are often the tales of other friendships found in his scholarly and personal endeavors. To interweave these two different realms can be troublesome, since the conventional notion of friendship that emphasizes equality and reciprocity seems unrealizable. The written words that emerge from the endeavors rarely return to those who gave them vivacity, and those who read the words seldom respond to the author relaying them. In other words, at least two kinds of *we* are expressed — the *we* that comprises those individuals described in the endeavors and the *we* to whom the descriptions are most immediately addressed.

To sustain these two kinds of *we* is more than a delicate balancing act. It implicates the reader as well as the author in a complex yet mysterious relation. The words that are written by Lingis and read by the audience often depict an as-if-you-are-there experience. Detailed descriptions and elaborate speculations help bring readers to a philosophical encounter so full of intrigue that it seems they and the author are on the same page.

Lingis is not entirely convinced. While the Foreword to *Abuses* admits that many of the chapters began as letters to friends, there lingers the sense that maybe the effort itself is a losing proposition. "It is hard to share something only with words on a silent page," he notes[11], but then adds that one of the tasks of philosophy is to speak for those who have been silenced. Certainly the subsequent chapters addressing guerillas, spiritual guides, prisoners, prostitutes, muscle builders, among others, illustrate this task.

The limitations here are nevertheless daunting and uneasy to articulate. After relating how he was quite sick for weeks in India and was helped to a hospital by a complete stranger who risked his life in the dark night of monsoon season, Lingis acknowledges momentary *we* that remains unforgettable. "He surely had no address but the sands; I would never see him again. I shall not cease seeing what it means to come to be bound with a bond that can never be broken or forgotten, what it means to become a brother."[12]

How a philosophical collage presents this ambivalent relation between author and reader can be seen in the essay "Lust." It introduces us to Calypso, an elaborate theater in Bangkok. One show features a pastiche of performers posing as Western pop stars—from Mae West to Marilyn Monroe and Farrah Fawcett— and closes with a dozen beautiful women wheeled onto the stage in an iron cage, liberated only after being inspected and picked by a handful of men. The Calypso, where so many performers are transvestites, is an antifeminist forum. It mocks our sense for role models and meaningful stories. Moreover, transvestite theater underscores the force of primal theater in general, which can be found in Harlem, Bali, Kyoto, and related sites that stand as a contrast to bourgeois or high theater where plot, true representation and cultural identity are prized.

Lingis then pictures what you—the tourist, the soldier on leave, the academic taking a break from a tedious conference, in other words, anyone delighting in this primal theater—could be experiencing. You see a Thai man doing a Thai woman's impersonations of Rock Hudson or Tom Cruise, or have Tina

Turner or Margaux Hemingway joining you at your table. Or you get lucky and entice Miss Thailand to your hotel room only to wind up disgusted when discovering what is hidden beneath the discarded dress.

The essay abruptly shifts to a concise account of libido. Whether one relies on the theory of Freud, Lacan or Lyotard, for many of us talking about sex remains talking about representations of cultural or personal identity, be it as self-knowledge, the true self or a contented self that emerges from internal conflicts. The problem, for Lingis, is that the idea of libido simply cannot do justice to the many features of primal theater, since it is not about libido but about lust—the lust in each of us. Peter Jackson indicts Lingis for offering a false ethnography about sexual identity, gay sexuality an ill-founded pansexualism of Thai culture. It is a curious charge. Nowhere in the chapter does the reader come across concerns about true or genuine sexual identity, whether of the Western tourist, cross-dressing performers at a Bangkok theater, or an ideal type of sexuality. On the contrary, for Lingis, this is not about finding one's true self. For lust invariably involves the power of the secret. "The walls of secrecy fragment our social identity. One is not the same person in sacred and in profane places, in crowds and behind closed doors...," Lingis observes, and adds, "Behind multiple generic identities, each of us builds his or her personal identity with inner walls of secrecy."[13]

As a collage essay, "Lust" interrupts the reader's focus with disparate descriptive and theoretical accounts. Yet it also establishes a *we* between the author and his audience, not to mention the *we* of those who are encountered, for in clarifying the distinctions between high and low theater, libido and lust, Lingis entreats us to consider a common element—the secrets harboring in each of us.

A Contested We

Secrets are often considered something internal. They are the stuff of intimate or private matters, glimpses into the real self, and thus deserve protection. To hold or harbor a secret involves the most basic moral issues, such as privacy rights, deceit, self-deception, loyalty. In contemporary circles the possible disclosure of someone's secret is usually an invitation to debate the limits of confidentiality or engage in the delights of gossip. Secrecy, according to Sissela Bok, is much richer of an experience than that. For it also extends one to domains of prohibition, stealth, intimacy, silence and the sacred.[14]

Secrets are poorly grasped when situated only in the private self. They are elements and forces having the potential to take us outside of ourselves. With secrets people reveal themselves to another. Telling someone else a secret about oneself need not always be seen as burdening others by means of comprising one's privacy or inner self. It can also be understood as a form of exposure.

For Lingis this exposure initiates not only a revelation about a private self. More importantly, it also provokes a contested *we*. He conceives the experience of being contested as one in which we sense or recognize the imperatives of others, the demands and solicitations that are more than appeals for personal gratification or consolation. In being contested we are more than the witnesses to the secrets of others; secrets are revealed not to anyone or everyone—they are only for you or me.

A secret shares etymological roots with discrete and secrete. Someone discretely reveals something to us, but in a way that secretes—that is, someone discharges or releases something of one's self to us. This is not the discharge of waste or extraneous material, but the expenditure of one's elements revealed or directed to another. To have someone secrete something of himself or herself to us has little to do with holding onto or passing along esoteric information—the secret is directed to us insofar as it contests us.

To be contested involves an encounter with or deliberation of the realities, torments, joys and imperatives of others. Thus the contest that is highlighted in, say, the agonistics of the Platonic dialog or the intellectual battle (i.e., attacking or defending claims, arguments and positions) of an academic seminar, provides only a partial account. According to Lingis, being contested is more richly understood in terms of exposure, affliction, bearing a weight, accompaniment, and vulnerability. These terms need not be construed negatively, nor must they act as references to a loss of identity or the pain of self-alienation. While being contested can expose or afflict oneself, this can be positive or affirmative insofar as exposure and affliction are experiences that introduce or awaken one to another. Unexpected knowledge, fresh insights, new truths and convictions are among the results of being contested.

Lingis observes:

> This is why it can happen that with the least glimpse at the other — the momentary glimpse at the slum child in the street as my car drives by, the momentary dull glint at the beggar's eyes in the dark as I head for the restaurant — I can feel arrested in my own intentions, contested...(and)
>
> The intruder comes as an intruder, and an authority, into the order of nature that my thought has represented in obedience to its own imperative...He or she approaches as the surface of another imperative. His approach contests my environment, my practical field, and my social arena.[15]

This sense of a contested *we* presented in collage form appears, for example, in "Violations". Lingis engages in what seems at first a conversation with himself. But the tones and features of each segment seem barely related. He begins with a philosopher's reflection on the centrality of language to the perennial question

51

over our ability to know others as speaking and thinking beings. The next paragraph is then completely indented, with a brief dismissal of language's power to reveal anything about another. As if posing questions from the history of philosophy by one of its wayward students, the essay reviews concisely the central thoughts of the Ancient Greeks, Hegel, Husserl on doctrines about human rationality, self-consciousness and self-worth that are central to philosophical discourse.

These reviews are punctuated with additional and completely indented passages that alternately sound cantankerous, irritable and derisive regarding the limitations inherent to these doctrines. How tedious it is to maintain personal identity, so trivializing and shallow is the moral basis for self-justifying sensibleness, Lingis complains. He then shifts focus by highlighting how we—his readers, himself—seek not those who confirm us but those who contest us, "who can show the stupidity in our thinking, who can send us back to really look."[16]

Yet there are times when we must look into ourselves and speak with our own voices rather than that of the institution or government that acts in our name. So much of our ordinary discourse involves justifying ourselves. Institutions and governments expect us to provide a justification for our actions, decisions, dietary habits, career moves and choices for love. In "To Know and to Acknowledge" Lingis contends that, "We owe no one a justification for our being there, for being alive, for craving to love. Not even God." We only owe an account to those we—directly or through our institutions and governments—have wronged. "We must recognize their shame, anger, and suffering and acknowledge the injustice, injury, and harm we have done to them. Only then do we make contact with who they are."[17]

The Imperative elaborates that nearly everyone has been an intruder at one time or another, however enthusiastic or reluctant. Much of human life is a nomadic adventure. Many cultures discourage a nomadic attitude, and Lingis, mindful of Foucault's studies of modern disciplinary societies, finds an emerging reticence to acknowledge or encourage individuals to experience themselves as intruders or outsiders. So it can be an eye-opener when he relates how in other cultures there is a tradition of the walkabout, in which an adolescent simply departs from the group for enough time to be contested by, but also companions with, "the other animals, the stars, and the spirits of the desert."[18]

Intermingling among you, I and we does not have the effect of bringing an audience together as if an essential core identity is discovered or recognized. The prevalent notion that violations are affronts or assaults upon one's sense of self-respect or integrity is undermined in this climate of contestation. It is not the self but the limits and barriers that we impose upon ourselves, in the name of personal or cultural identity, that become violated. For Lingis, what happens to the ego is of secondary importance. Of primary concern is how violations give rise to laughter, tears, joy, grief and erotic play. These elements bring out the most intense forms of communication.

To discuss and scrutinize these elements philosophically encompasses a medley of experiences and insights. Hence the essay as collage is accentuated with glimpses of a priest dropping two bottles of smuggled liquor in an airport lobby, a woman dancing in the streets of Salvador, a street urchin daring to talk with the Brazilian singer Edson Cordeiro, and sundry others who communicate to Lingis new ways of laughing over all the serious things overburdening the self. By the essay's closing, then, the contested *we* is ultimately not about violation but liberation: "We seek to be freed from the carapace of ourselves."[19]

The Task Before Us?

Numerous essays of Lingis conclude with an account of someone setting out on a task. An immigrant sitting by the road fixing a predigital watch, a transvestite stopping by a café table to entertain some tourists, a nurse attending to a cholera-stricken child, friends and family offering solace to the dying, a youth in Central America preparing for his execution by the government's thugs, peasants helping a widow bury her husband, are among the final images Lingis leaves his readers.

These images are then juxtaposed with the possible tasks awaiting Lingis or the reader. For example, after observing the funeral procession in an impoverished Central American village, Lingis admits that he must return to students in America, with their luxuriant tastes for computers, CD players, designer clothes and colleagues, with their voracious appetites to explain every organism and decipher every biological code. Then he abruptly moves from the plush classroom setting to a chilly and sparse room not far from the procession, a room awaiting tender exchanges with a peasant. Thus *Abuses* ends as if giving the reader the task to consider which environment fosters a facile or intense *we*.

Two other books close by featuring chance or once-in-a-lifetime encounters that momentarily bring humans together.[20] Variances in cultural identity, psychological profile, political or religious affiliation, wealth, sex or age can neither explain nor prevent these encounters. Street urchins, old women, philosophers' words, surprise lovers, dying patients are among the innumerable contacts that introduce tasks we pursue or avoid. We either turn away and retreat or respond to them and come upon moments of brotherhood, kinship, collaboration, friendship and accompaniment and the unexpected tasks arising in these moments.

In the spirit of the collage, Lingis often concludes with scarcely a personal comment. He lets the contrasting images, as if echoing the photographs that intersperse these books, speak on their own. But like the analysis of artistic collages by Rosenberg, it does not follow that the author's voice and thought are entirely absent. They too are parts of the collage, alternating tones, perspectives, emotions and ideas. That it remains up to the reader, not the author, to draw some meaning or conclusion from the juxtapositions does not entail an open-ended playfulness or dismantling the text. Rather, it asks to consider which sort of *we* does the reader experience as a reader, and as an individual.

Is this the only task for the reader—to make sense of a philosophical collage? Lingis acknowledges a sense of helplessness over generating a more practical or productive relation between author and reader. Regardless of the images of those carrying out their tasks, he realizes that we may not have the compassion of the nurse, the courage of the imprisoned youth, the brazenness of the transvestite, or the loyalty of the peasants. Yet he does believe that these images—their stories, faces and bodies—still have the power to arouse passion, one that brings the author together with readers while contesting them and himself at the same time. It is with these senses of first person plural that Lingis ends: "Because we do not bribe our way into their cells, tear off our clothes, opening all our orifices to them on the stiff cots or cement floors of their cells, our sensuality is constricted, asphyxiated, and ashamed."[21]

The Liberating Element of Collage

While Lingis is a staunch proponent of phenomenology, it is through his studies of postmodern thinkers that he engages a revised form of phenomenology so that the themes highlighting postmodern discussion become stepping-stones for the central themes of Lingis's works discussed here. Rather than focus on constructions of social identity, pitfalls of reason, the instability of texts or the nefarious webs of power in personal and political realms, he relies on thinkers such as Nietzsche and Bataille— two stalwarts for many postmodern dispositions—in order to discover, articulate and understand forms of *we* that exemplify joy, mastery, gift, sacrifice and innocence found among numerous figures from many lands. What they exemplify has little to do with relativism of values or interpreting bodies as if they were texts. These accounts of first person plural instead show how inexplicably certain passions, imperatives and values seem ever present.

For Lingis the positive forms of *we* also illuminate thought. Thoughts do not only arise from the meditations carried on inside one's head or the exchange and refinement of ideas that shape public and rational discourse. Thoughts involve experiences in which a *we* is formed. Hence Lingis points out in "The Rational and the Required", the last chapter of *The Imperative*, "Thought itself is not produced by deliberation about how to form concepts and how to connect them; insights come as gifts from a contact with things where we give ourselves completely to them and they to us."[22]

Comprised of such gifts, a collage can become a guide for a philosophical essay and project. With an essay as collage, Lingis is able to establish a *we*—collaborative as well as contested and adversarial—with his readers.

Yet collage is also a project. In his writings this project emphasizes the task of being awakened or enlightened to new truths and realities without any reassurance that our common truths remain tenable or justifiable. Loss of this reassurance is for many of us daunting and inhibiting. In the spirit of a collage, however, this loss is liberating. It frees me from my stubborn convictions; it liberates you from your useful conventions; it helps Lingis and his readers escape their shared stupidities.

From such liberating moments new forms of *we* are discovered or created. To encounter them in a philosophical way, Lingis presents a conceptual lens and critical apparatus for current and subsequent generations of students and scholars to experience or examine the elements that define first person plural. Such defining moments will, on occasion, arise from a collective. More frequently they will speak of a collage.

Notes

1. See, for example, Richard Rorty's "Who Are We? Moral Universalism and Economic Triage", *Diogenese* 173 (Spring 1996) and David Palumbo-Lius's subsequent rejoinder in "Awful Patriotism", *diacritics* 29/1 (1999). For this chapter, first person plural will be italicized when referring to uses or meanings in Lingis's writings, and will not be italicized when appearing as a commonplace referent to those reading or discussing them. This distinction is not always as precise as we could like, of course.

2. Alphonso Lingis, *Dangerous Emotions* (Berkeley, CA: University of California Press, 2000), 181.

3. Lingis, *The Imperative*, 42-43.

4. Harold Rosenberg, "Collage: Philosophy of Put-Togetherness" in *Collage: Critical Views*, ed. Katherine Hoffman (Ann Arbor, MI: UMI Research Press, 1989), 36. Amy Lyford makes a fascinating case for seeing the early works in collage as aesthetic but also as political events in response to the French government's rather gruesome treatment of casualties from World War I. See "The Aesthetics of Dismemberment", *Cultural Critique* 46 (1999), 37-56. Also see Lingis, *Deathbound Subjectivity*, pp. 79-80, "For us the category of collage gives a post-classical idea of an artwork. The first thing it says is that it represents nothing and means nothing...Here the contingent, the insignificant, the ephemeral, the broken, the haphazard, is not composed but just set forth, affirmed."

5. Lingis, *Foreign Bodies*, 162-163.

6. Lingis, *The Imperative*, 3.

7. Lingis, *Foreign Bodies*, viii.

8. Alphonso Lingis, *Abuses* (Berkeley: University of California Press, 1994), 33.

9. Lingis, *Dangerous Emotions*, 101.

10. Lingis, *The Community of Those Who Have Nothing in Common*, 157-158.

11. Lingis, *Abuses*, vii.

12. Lingis, *The Community…*, 159.

13. Lingis, *Abuses*, 125, 127.

14. Sissela Bok, *Secrets: On the Ethics of Concealment and Revelation* (New York: Pantheon, 1982).

15. Lingis, *The Community…* 28, 33.

16. Lingis, *Dangerous Emotions*, 90.

17. Lingis, *The First Person Singular*, 116.

18. Lingis, *The Imperative,* 166.

19. Lingis, *Dangerous Emotions*, 101.

20. Lingis, *Foreign Bodies*, 224, and *The Community…* 164.

21. Lingis, *Dangerous Emotions*, 191.

22. Lingis, *The Imperative*, 221.

Chapter Four

Silence, Speech, Thought

People's voices are like found poetry—raw, uncrafted, imperfect. Still, we do them the greatest justice when we choose carefully and get out of the way.
Kelley Benham[1]

How Indecent

As with the face, it is uncertain whether silence began as a noun or verb. Maybe it was first an adjective, a property assigned to that which makes no sound. Mystics and visionaries assert something more—silence can be an important daily moment or an occasional and intense experience. Musicians such as John Cage and communication scholars such as Deborah Tannen see silence as a flip side, the essential shadow or the irreplaceable twin of what we hear, listen to, express or speak.

For all his loquaciousness, Socrates' friends often recalled his ability to sit or stand in one area, neither move nor speak, oblivious to the cacophony of the agora, while seeming to carry on a quiet conversation with himself. Frederic Gros asserts that walking and silence provide fundamental philosophical moments. We walk amid the silence of woodlands, hot summer afternoons, deep snowfalls, early morning and the dark of night. "In the silence of the walk, when you end up losing the use of words because by then you are doing nothing but walk...in that silence you hear better, because you are finally hearing what has no vocation to be retranslated, recoded, reformatted."[2] Kant, Rousseau, Thoreau and Nietzsche were among many thinkers who sought solitary and silent walks as an essential part of their lives. St Theresa of Avila and Hildegaard von Bingen, regardless of their eloquence with words, images and sounds, found silence to be a fundamental mode of the spiritual life and one's relation to the divine. Monks take a vow of silence, as do members of subversive, rebellious or secret societies. Journalists, anthropologists and travel writers are among the various genres attempting to present other people's stories while minimizing their own voices.

Two enduring aspects of silence arise between a writer and reader. There is first an extended gap from when the author writes to a year or two later when the reader quietly reads the essay or chapter. The second silence derives from the author when withdrawing his or her own voice in order to retell or represent the stories of others, via experience, hearsay or scholarship. Contrary to skeptics who indict Lingis with a none-too-subtle exploitation by posing as medium for stories of obscure people in third world locales, he is quite alert to his precarious position.

Whether relaying his own memories or the recollections of the numerous writers that appear in his accounts of strangers and foreign lands, Lingis reminds the reader that his position as author, scholar and traveler presses with cautious hesitation. He admits that the people he meets are unsure if they will have enough money the next week to feed themselves or their family, whereas he can simply sign a credit card and indulge his appetites any day. He realizes that some of his new-found friends will return to hovels and desolate camps for the night while he can easily stay at a three-star hotel a mile or two away.

What brings disparate people together often has little to do with a common language, resources or heritage. Something before language or shared commonality sometimes occurs. Lingis finds that humans frequently recognize one another in their joy, curses, laughter and tears. These emotions are not after-effects of thoughts or passive responses to a situation. They are positive or creative. They have us bless our good fortunes, curse the despots, laugh at ourselves and bear tears for one another's sorrows. They move us to respond, explore and inquire.

In his words, these dangerous emotions "break through the packaging and labeling of things that make our environment something only scanned and skimmed over. They are forces with which we impact on nature, which we had perused only as the text of the world. They are forces that seek out and engage reality."[3] Laughter, tears, joy and sorrow are also forces that initially elude articulation or the self-awareness that is expected of rational or deliberative actions.

Jill LeBlanc contends that silence is an affirmative act rather than merely a negative response that bears no meaning. Being silent or silencing oneself often conveys as much insight as the proper use of words and tones. For mystics, silence is one of the essential modes of communication and understanding. LeBlanc outlines the varieties of speech acts where staying silent in certain contexts expresses loyalty to a captured comrade, conveys insight to friends or family, connotes a quiet laugh about one's own foibles or before possible danger, or quietly succumbs to the fates. Silence also connects the believer to a deity, a fighter to a cause, or a lover to the beloved. In any event, in LeBlanc's words, "The meaningful silence that cannot be vocalized is a case of keeping silent about a specific topic because you cannot say anything about it."[4] Such silence is an invaluable response to an encounter where a speech might act as a betrayal.

The Community of Those Who Have Nothing in Common is a concise and varied meditation on the forces of silence that extends LeBlanc's key points to the meaningfulness of a silence among rebels, mystics, savages, the insane, those facing exile or death. There is a curious feature in silence that Lingis highlights in the case of torture. Those administering the torture seek to erase the voices of its captives (forcing a confession is just a ruse) with its pain-inducing machinery, but the victims of torture attempt to hold their tongue out of loyalty and honor for their fellow victims.

Lingis observes, "In the resistance in his body, the torture victim hears the silence of the suffering from which one could no longer protect the others, and of their anger, from which one could not expect anything."[5] The book closes with observations about humans' recognition of one another, be it based on a common language, economy, religion, shared interest, biological or familial lineage. Beyond this recognition, Lingis describes associations that have "nothing" in common. Perhaps their respective countries are at war with one another, their backgrounds or religions are from different realms, or the languages are so different that verbal communication is impossible.

Five years before the publication of *Excesses*, Lingis delineated three forms of association. They are identification, associational synopsis and the simple recognition of alterity (otherness). In his subsequent books he illustrates and reexamines them. Each form incorporates its own relation to language, symbols, mutual respect, intentions, justice and sensual experience. With Levinas's ideas on alterity as a departure point, Lingis contends the third form is actually a kind of disassociation. Here one does not focus on similarities and differences with the other. Instead one is contested by or responds to another. Lingis calls this "extreme dissociation, this departure that leaves traces that mean nothing and indicate nothing, that disturb, deserved above all the name of association."[6]

One instance of this dissociation begins in the darkness of night in southern India. Lingis is quite sick, an infection seems to partially paralyze some of his limbs. He needs to reach the hospital in Madras, 65 miles away, but has no guide. By chance a young man with a canoe spots Lingis and rows him to a nearby port. There the young man ensures and entrusts other vendors that they help Lingis to catch a rickshaw and then a bus to Madras. Through this venture the young man alternated moments of silence with chatter about what Lingis took to be accounts of the surroundings, the canoe, the darkness and tales told many times. Mostly the young man stayed focused on the mission. As he gazed upon the surroundings and checked the skies for a possible storm, Lingis became convinced that the young man would risk his life if the sickly traveler's own safety was threatened.

In this context, Lingis confesses: "How indecent to speak of such things in the anonymous irresponsibility of a writing he cannot read and a tongue he cannot understand!" [7]

Gratitude and Silence

Gratitude does not rank among the seven cardinal virtues. It has nevertheless received numerous endorsements as essential to leading a good and happy life. Given the status of pride or hubris as the vice that poses the most dangerous catalyst for becoming tempted by the other vices, gratitude is often promoted as a worthy antidote and prevention to the excesses of pride. One problem with gratitude is that it can be embarrassingly overused, risking shallowness or triviality. Acceptance speeches cite thanks for everyone else's contributions, from manager and agent to one's own children and pets. Several industries thrive by providing cards for Mother's and Father's Day to help those of us who are too inept or busy to articulate a sincere thank you with pen and paper.

A second problem concerns the nature of gratitude. Andre Comte-Sponville contends that gratitude is an expression of thanks and respect for forces behind our accomplishments. But how do we know that these forces were not simply a matter of good fortune, poor luck, a twist of fate or a bad draw of the cards? Comte-Sponville contends that the object of gratitude, similar to his support of the target of loyalty, is sometimes less important than the fact that one conveys gratitude as an extension of humility. That is whatever our accomplishments and our satisfaction in pursuing them, articulating a sense of gratitude shows an appreciation of influences outside one's own self. Furthermore, he sees gratitude as a gesture that brings us closer to the truth and momentarily frees us from the anxiety of our mortality. In his words, "Gratitude is the enjoyment of eternity."[8]

Comte-Sponville's eloquent account of gratitude addresses a paradoxical concern found in Lingis's perspective. Generally we assume that those who write or speak on behalf of others are using their speech to convey the stories of others and the author's own thoughts about their stories (although the temptation to arrogance and dominance should also be granted). Lingis shifts the focus. Suppose the author admits a gratitude that cannot be expressed in any substantive way? Perhaps gratitude sometimes has nothing to do with the enjoyment of eternity but a forgetfulness of joy itself.

The essay "Reticence" is a meditation on the limits of language when faced with inexpressible experiences and senses of gratitude. The central discussion is sandwiched by two passages. The opening page states in a one-sentence paragraph, "But gratitude—thoughtfulness—can also silence talk." The last page of the essay has another single sentence paragraph, "Yet the extreme experiences, the events for which we are most grateful, are harbored in silence."[9]

Between these two paragraphs Lingis suspends his own silence and discusses the tensions and surprises of things that grab out attention and the capability of our language to communicate them. There are experiences of voluptuous pleasure, ecstatic wonder or compelling visions which elude conventional accounts, other than maybe "O Wow!" or "Awesome." In addition, such moments bring about an effacement of one's self. In his view, visitors open themselves to the Grand Canyon's grandeur, divers immerse themselves in the deep seas, or hikers approach the giant sequoias with the effect of diminishing their sense of self. Not in any negative way such as alienation or self-loathing, but in an affirmative way that celebrates a natural wonder, the ocean's dark powers or a tree so large that it contains its own little ecosystems.

Understandably, the relation between a writer, words and his or her own relation to those words is murky. A reader of Lingis might find him also treading murky territory. In the various encounters one has with a stranger, often one forgets one's status, wealth, personal identity. These ephemeral and memorable encounters transform or possess us to the point of emptiness, including the language to express that emptiness. As Lingis observes, "The most intense joys we are given empty the mind, extinguish the ego, and silence the greedy work of words."[10]

Is not the writer of this sentence, who has produced some 20 books, inadvertently succumbing to the greedy work of words?

Telling True Stories

Peter Jackson decided to cease his silence on Lingis's ideas in fear that others might think he condones Lingis's travel writings and, specifically, his essay on lust in Bangkok, Thailand. He finds the American thinker's stylistic lucidity to be a disturbing seduction for a reader who does not know any better. Jackson does know better. He ascribes to Lingis's travelogues traits of voyeurism and exploitation. They are symptoms of a privileged academic and, in Jackson's words, "...just another angst-ridden colonizer feeling guilty about his power rather than a liberator."[11] Jackson's indictment seems eerie to professors who have assigned *Abuses* for their courses. Not one professor has reported of a single student reading "Lust" only to conclude that Lingis is a guilt-ridden colonizer.

A historian of male eroticism in Thailand, Jackson is also known for his ethnographic studies of a specific male, *kathoey*, a hybrid of a transgendered and transsexual male. He accuses Lingis of seeing men's bodies in Thailand as projects of "his theoretical fantasies of psychoanalytic pansexuality,"[12] indicating that Lingis is blind to his own narrow touristic and Orientalist biases. Indeed, he sarcastically bemuses, "One is left to wonder whether Lingis was able to tell the difference between a kathoey and a Thai Woman."[13]

It seems to be a matter of indifference in this accusation that the phrase or concept of "psycholanalytic pansexuality" does not anywhere appear in Lingis's discussion about lust and Thailand. Nor is there any concern that Lingis is not attempting an ethnographical account of gender identities in these Bangkok theaters. Lingis rather finds wonder in the playfulness, innocuous joy, creative poses and disguises that are anchored to the erotic desires and restless imaginations.

As a contrast to the associations found in ordinary society in which we exchange representations and symbols of libido with one another[14], Lingis focuses on the laughter and surprise that arises in these Thai theaters rather than the deep truths of sexual identity. Jackson completely neglects this fascination Lingis conveys to the reader. For it is not about what is transparent, but what still tantalizes as hidden. In Lingis's account of this theater where there is so much daring, "Is it transposing or releasing, subverting or trumpeting lust? That is its secret. The power to keep its secrets is the secret of its power."[15]

Lingis is also indicted, in terms of a rhetorical question, on why he is perpetuating a "persistent ethnocentrism of Western philosophy" that leads him to "construct his fairy tale account of Thailand, describing a myth of a place that exists nowhere but on the pages of his book?" Jackson's answer: Because the myth fulfills Lingis's theoretical fantasies.[16] Lingis's anecdotes and observations of Thai theater say nothing about lust or the performers, only inadvertent revelations that Lingis merely imposes his intellectual biases upon the topic or experience. These biases reveal his unstated commitments to fundamental themes in Western thought. Unfortunately, juries listening to this charge can only guess which aspect of Western philosophy

Lingis has imposed upon those he meets in other cultures and worlds. Jackson offers no specifics.

Jackson's charges amount to either circular reasoning or an *ad hominem* dressed in academic jargon. The circular reasoning appears in Jackson's claiming that Lingis projects his own biases but Jackson can only know this from Lingis's writings. In Jackson's formulation, we know the bias of the written work but only because the writer unwittingly conveys the bias. Some independent frame of reference is needed, but Jackson provides none—except for references to his own writings. The *ad hominem* charge of a Western philosophical projection has become such a commonplace that Lingis's possible rejoinder might seem old-fashioned. His writings often do admit to a philosophical bad habit. They are focused on questioning his own philosophical and social conventions in light of his encounters and research. His descriptions, historical accounts and vivid portrayals attempt to highlight the truths of other stories.

The Thought Behind Their Voices

Daniel Dennett claims that, "In the end, you're not taking any philosopher seriously until you ask whether or not what they say is *right*."[17] Dennett does not mean that you have to agree with the philosopher, just that what is said or written sounds plausible, seems to have happened, offers a sense of reality, has credibility, could be true or provides a worthy insight or paradox. In telling philosophical stories, Lingis exemplifies Dennett's point by finding what is right and real about the stories told and retold. His "as-if-you-were there" portraits introduce unexpected characters, unusual environments, eccentric celebrations or rituals and surprise twists or encounters. They give the reader the impression that these depictions represent so many counterexamples. Counterexamples to what? To those beliefs and attitudes the reader has often found to be conventional, traditional, civil or meaningful.

No doubt passions drive many of these accounts. Courage, laughter, sorrow, love, torment, joy are among the passions featured in the stories told and retold. This point should not obscure how Lingis also studies the thought behind their voices. His reliance on scholars, from anthropology to zoology, illuminates how the deeds and twists of their stories make sense, have a respect for reality, anticipate possible consequences, are reflective of or a resistance to the way things have been done before, and possess an acute awareness of their immediate circumstances and the possibilities decided upon.

Consider how *Trust* unfolds. The reader is introduced to a remote desert locale called "Araouane."[18] Several guides or helpers are named. The traveler is caught off guard by the hot and desolate sands. It is windy, with tiny bits of salt or dust constantly nipping at one's face. At times in the Sahara one becomes convinced that the universe is made only of sand and sky. The chief guide, Izzah, continually informs Lingis and his readers about destinations of animals or humans who have recently traversed the same landscape. Upon arrival in Araouane, the guest is welcomed by the villagers. They take him to the herds of goats and sheep, local schools, places for slaughtering the animals, and the house of the mullah where prayers, readings of the Koran and extended silences are part of everyday life. Izzah then shows a nearby town that is at least 2000 years old.

Lingis updates the reader on how Araouane's sacred elements have been overwhelmed by an onslaught of oil businesses wishing to transform the entire area. To develop this thesis, he retraces several historical developments that lead to the current moment, even as far back as 1000 CE when the great warriors "The Taureg" dominated this part of the Sahara. Suddenly the reader visualizes Izzah, through the eyes of Lingis, stopping five times a day to pray. This sacred moment is then juxtaposed with the recent emergence of oil wells and tankers in the background desacralizing the life and culture of Araouane.

Seeing the story of Izzah, the reader also learns the stories of his people, including their traditions and conflicts, the immediate options—be it resistance, resignation or compromise—due to the likely dominance of oil industries. Lingis closes the essay with his own reticence by speculating on the nature of the sacred, not just on a small section of the Sahara desert, but the place of earthly life in the cosmos and the decomposition of human life in that scenario. In this case, no direct conclusion is drawn.

Lingis's silence here appears as a kind of gratitude to readers in having them draw their own conclusions. In this case the silence is a communicative act. It opens the space in which the truth of the stories and voices told and retold is conveyed from writer to reader. In these uncrafted and imperfect stories, to borrow from Kelley Benham, the truths and thoughts behind these voices are encountered. At such times Lingis steps aside. This silent gesture attempts to offer the greatest moment of justice.

Notes

1. Kelley Benham, "Hearing Our Subjects' Voices: Quotes and Dialogues", in *Telling True Stories*, ed. Mark Kramer and Wendy Call (New York: Plume/Penguin, 2007), 107.

2. Frederic Gros, *A Philosophy of Walking*, trans. John Howe (New York: Verso, 2014), 62.

3. Lingis, *Dangerous Emotions*, 78.

4. Jill LeBlanc, "The Act of Silence", *Philosophy Today* (Fall, 1995), 326.

5. Lingis, *The Community of Those Who Have Nothing in Common*, 152.

6. Alphonso Lingis, "Association" in *Analecta Husserliana, The Human Being in Action.* Ed. A-T Tymieniecka (Dordrecht: D. Reidel, 1978).

7. Lingis, *The Community...*, 159.

8. Andre Comte-Sponville, *A Small Treatise on the Great Virtues*, trans. Catherine Temerson (New York: Holt, 2001).133.

9. Lingis, *Trust*, 199.

10. Ibid., 198.

11. Peter A. Jackson, "Spurning Alphonso Lingis' Thai 'Lust': The Perils of a Philosopher at Large", *Intersections: Gender, History and Culture in the Asian Context* (Issue 2, May 1999),4.

12. Ibid., 7.

13. Ibid., 5.

14. Lingis, *Abuses*, 123.

15. Ibid., 124.

16. Jackson, "'Spurning Alphonso Lingis..."

17. Daniel C. Dennett, *Intuition Pumps and Other Tools for Thinking* (New York: W.W. Norton, 2013), 426.

18. Lingis, *Trust*, 3-12.

Chapter Five

Knowledge via The Passions, from Courage to Laughter

"Life as a means to knowledge"—with this principle in one's heart one can live not only boldly but even gaily, and laugh gaily, too. And who knows how to laugh anyway and live well if he does not first know a good deal about war and victory?
Nietzsche[1]

Love Junkies

Lingis presents the story of Australians Wayne and Cheryl through several venues. Under the title "Love Junkies", there is a multimedia presentation that combines music, moving images or intermittent slides, background lights with Lingis disguising himself while reading his observations directly and indirectly related to the presentation's title and surrounding sounds and sights. One university promoted the talk with the line "Have you ever loved that much? Have you ever been loved that much?" This is an intellectual spectacle.

A second venue appears as a straightforward interview. Lingis records his conversations with Wayne and Cheryl. With the curiosity of an inquisitive journalist rather than the cynicism of a political reporter, he poses questions not as accusations or suspicions, but as solicitations for facts, anecdotes and recollections. The responses are elaborate and quite candid. Wayne and Cheryl acknowledge the ups and downs of their lives, before and while they became lovers. They opened up to the interviewer and his potential audience.

The third venue features Lingis's own perspective as illuminated in the "Love Junkies" chapter in *Trust*[2]. Here Lingis incorporates many of the snippets and insights garnered from

71

the interviews and presents them anew through reflections about courage, laughter and the insights that passions provide. As with many essays, Lingis begins with the focus on the first person singular. This is not happenstance. Lingis contends that to discuss *you* in a philosophical way has often been dominated by two perspectives. The Hegelian version is that we address you in order to seek recognition of ourselves. I need you to confirm my freedom or validate my authority or sense of self. The second tradition of addressing you has been to engage in a moral justification of our respective lives. We prepare to excuse or accuse one another of our guarded successes or failings and how they rank in terms of good will, sincerity or contributions to a happier society.

Lingis offers a third option. To address *you* is also a kind of exposure, vulnerability or fundamental respect. When saying *you* to a child, sibling, spouse, lover or stranger, we momentarily forget about ourselves and are simply focused on others before us. In his words, "To approach you with respect is to expose my seriousness of purpose to the flash fires of your laughter, expose my cheerfulness to the darkness of your grief, let you put your blessing on my discomfiture and suffering, expose myself to the shock waves or your curses."[3] In this light he deploys *you* to address Wayne or Cheryl as if he were sending a personal letter that recounts their story through a philosophical lens.

Obviously the reader is also in the essay's scope, as the essay opens with a direct photo of Wayne and Cheryl sitting closely on a ledge. Lingis introduces Cheryl, born a male whose foster parents named Paul. They were confused when Paul shifted to embrace the body and mannerisms of a woman and took on the name Cheryl. In any event, they appreciated Cheryl's partner Wayne. Wayne was always in trouble with the law. His father had a mean streak, placing Wayne into an orphan's home when he turned 7 years old.

In a mix of a matter-of-fact tone and terse observations from

Lingis, the reader encounters the unpredictable moments in the lives of Wayne and Cheryl. Each committed enough petty crimes or violent offenses to earn a lengthy stay in the Australian prison "Long Bay gaol." Both have had addictions and tested positive for HIV. Cheryl has been raped in the prison. Some of the attackers did it not for sexual pleasure as much as catching the deadly virus from Cheryl in order to flirt more closely with their own death. Hearing that the two men soon died, Cheryl shrugged her shoulders and attended their funeral services in order to forget.

Cheryl can be mischievous and sneaky. Prisoners and guards often keep an eye on her for possible shenanigans. Wayne does not mince words, nor does he back down from a physical brawl when challenged. He is quite skilled in handling himself with his fists or a weapon. That is one reason he has been in jail a good part of his life. Wayne does have enough patience to accept an occasional misguided threat to him, but that courtesy is not extended to anyone who dares to harm Cheryl.

Wayne is also an autodidact, self-taught in computers so well that his fellow inmates relied on him for instruction or technical assistance. The essay closes with Cheryl's recollection of how she faked a robbery at a McDonald's store in order to get arrested so she could return to jail and be with Wayne. When retelling this to Wayne or Lingis, the reader is caught by the concluding image of Cheryl "shrieking with drag queen laughter."[4]

The Laughable Animal

Since the time of Plato and Aristotle, courage has always been considered to be an indisputable primary virtue. It is the virtue that makes other virtues possible or meaningful. The passion that energizes courage has been a recurring feature of folklore, political movements and religious revolutions, as well as some favorite novels and films. If a child asks what courage is, we can readily cite a variety of examples, pointing to those with holidays named after them, film stars like Batman, Spiderman or Jason Bourne who generate box office hits, or the heroes that are featured in literature or legend.

Laughter has a more salacious reputation. Plato and Aristotle warned against the laughter that showed loss of rational control (such as a convulsive or belly laugh) or relied on malice and the ridicule of others as if they were inferior beings. Given its intellectual and civic aspects, wit was the ideal form of humor. In religious circles earthly laughter could weaken the soul's focus on duties of worship and service. Laughter's nature and effects have been debated in a range of human modes, including madness, ecstasy, absurdity and sage-like insight. It is more than restraining oneself in the proper environment—its danger lies in bringing about the temporary forgetfulness of oneself.

What makes humor a remarkable passion, according to Anca Parvulescu, lies in its power to alter humans as well as be subject to so many shifting taboos.[5] Interweaving the writings of such desperate writers as Kafka, Kristeva, Beckett, Hobbes, Sartre and visual presentations of the laughing face by artists and photographers, she examines two directions for understanding the significance of laughter. The first and conventional one is that humans are the only animal that laughs. Laughter and the sense of humor it evokes is a cognitive act. It involves evaluating our fellow humans and recognizing an absurdity or incongruity, or the distance of superiority among other members of our species.

The second direction is influenced by Georges Bataille. Parvulescu contends that Bataille makes the case for believing that we are also the only laughable animal. Even the various portraits of hilarious faces she presents in her analysis spark suspicion. Mouth wide open, missing teeth, hysterical looking eyes, freakish turn of the lips, snarling nose, sinister eyebrows. We do not laugh at animal faces, unless they are merely projections of human plights. We are the animal that laughs because we are the only animal ridiculous enough to be laughed about.

Bataille claims laughter is an excessive force. It is not directly related to satisfying essential needs for survival or procreation. It is a passion that comes by surprise, threatens loss of self-control and thrives on mockery of conventions and authorities. This power of laughter is not to be condemned. To the contrary, says Bataille, much laughter can be seen as a liberating and contagious force:

> From one end to the other end of human life which is our lot, the consciousness of the paucity of stability, even of the profound lack of all true stability, liberates the enchantment of laughter...If a group of people laugh at an absent-minded gesture, or at a sentence revealing an absurdity, there passes within them a current of intense communication. Each betraying the error of immutable isolation. It emerges from itself in a sort of easy flash; it opens itself at the same time to the contagion of a wave, which rebounds, for those who laugh together become like the waves of the sea—there no longer exists between them any partition as long as the laughter lasts; they are no more separate than are two waves, but their unity is as undefined, as precarious as that of the agitation of the waters.[6]

In light of Bataille's direction, Parvulescu speculates on a community of laughter. It could be anchored to a passion that communicates a "yawning gap" in which the laughter dissolves momentarily the separation between one and another. Unlike Aristotle's emphasis on moderation, Parvulescu envisions a laughter that is inherently excessive to the point that "to die laughing" remains a meaningful hyperbole. She also acknowledges the potential paradox of this community of laughter. In her words, "Bataille thinks about laughter in order to come to understand the workings of community, and he thinks about community in order to try to understand laughter."[7]

For this reason laughter is linked to so many areas of human community—eros, joy, death, love, communication—for they are also the objects of laughter that spur transgression.

Doing Time in Australia

Prisons are unique to human beings. No other animal constructs an impenetrable and inescapable fortress to house other living members of their own species. No other species forces members of one sex to be permanently residing away from and having no physical contact with the other sex. No other creatures on this planet will make their fellow creatures submit to arbitrary examination of all their bodily orifices, live among squalor and constant danger, tolerate incessant boredom or the psychological torture of 23-hour days in solitary confinement. By any measure, doing time raises questions about the violations of the 8th Amendment that prohibits cruel and unusual punishment. Prisons are extreme circumstances. Could they possibly prepare the workings of community that contribute to an understanding of laughter?

In his 16-page "Love Junkies"[8] essay on the story of Wayne and Cheryl in an Australian prison, Lingis refers to their laughter or humor at least seven times. In some of their anecdotes the reader finds "funny peculiar and funny ha-ha." (113). Wayne is noted for his dry sense of humor, Cheryl a charming and muffled giggle, and when together they are much like lovers through most of the human world: "They have locked the door and pulled the drapes so that their laughter may be uninhibited, one, and undivided." (120) Regardless of our accomplishments or misfortunes, much of what we have done will, in Lingis's own mockery of our self-importance, "soon be covered with graffiti and pigeon shit." As with Cheryl, who has no idea why she was adopted, at certain moments most of us will toss up our hands in resignation and can only laugh. (123).

Borrowing from Bataille borrowing from Nietzsche, Lingis

sees laughter as a creative excess, an expenditure without the expectation of anything in return. Laughter often integrates with courage, lust, silence and honesty. What distinguishes Lingis's perspective is the earthiness and vulnerable basis of laughter's functions. "In laughter," he observes, "we are transparent to one another, the peals of laughter not expressions of an I or a you, spreading like waves about a pebble dropped into a lake, with no more individuality than waves." (120)

Lingis does not sugar coat the lives of Wayne and Cheryl. He does recognize in the stories they tell certain wits and attitudes that deserve our philosophical attention. Wayne has a temper, but is widely respected by inmates and the guards for his courage and candor. He and Cheryl expect complete honesty from one another, and often worry when they are apart for merely a couple of hours. Wayne has a hierarchy of associations. Of the thousands of people he's met in and outside prison, he says about one hundred would call him a friend where he would say only 60 he regards as a friend. Then there are the 20 with whom he trusts. And from that 20, "...there's five that I would die for or kill for." (118)

This is most evident in Wayne's love for Cheryl. Since everyone in prison knows this, no one messes with Cheryl. She and Wayne are quite attentive to the medical well-being of their fellow inmates by encouraging better treatment of those who are HIV positive, particularly those dying from AIDS. They frequently write to politicians seeking better resources for educating the prisoners. Cheryl keeps reminding prison officials to take care of the facilities, be it painting, cleaning or repairing.

The many stories surrounding the lives of Wayne and Cheryl call our attention to familiar disputes about love, honesty, courage, gratitude and a heartfelt sense of good cheer. The environment of these disputes is not the classroom, but a prison. They recognize the absurd and threatening aspects of their situation and the ups and downs of their lives. "Shit happens," they occasionally remind themselves. Yet at the end they laugh about how lucky they are to have found each other, to love and probably die together.

When Wayne and Cheryl first entered the prison, this most inhuman form of daily life, they could not have expected their stories would convey an insight or paradox of what awaited them. No one could have anticipated the knowledge to be gained from their passions, however constricted or short-lived. In the story of Wayne and Cheryl, no sage could have predicted that in this most inhuman environment one would experience elements of a humaneness of the future.

Are Virtues in Excess Still Virtuous?

Throughout his writings Lingis describes and depicts virtuous persons and deeds. At least that's how proponents of virtue ethics might see it. Of the cardinal seven virtues, for example, moments of courage, justice, love or charity are illuminated through anecdotes and characters presented in his articles and books. Other frequent contenders for virtue status, such as compassion, care or honesty, are readily visible in his encounters or scholarly reflections.

By conventional versions of virtue ethics, however, there is no reason to claim that Lingis embraces a virtue ethic. Most endorsements of virtue ethics emphasize an integral self, one guided by reason and civic duty. One becomes virtuous through moderation and an on-going practice of the self. Develop and maintain habits that help one embody the virtues and contribute to the general happiness. Institutions, from family and education to government and military, contribute to the social good by encouraging a life of virtue among individuals.

"Virtue" stems from the Greek term for excellence, but also contains the root "virile" that refers to masculinity. For Plato, Aristotle, Augustine and the major supporters of virtue ethics, a virtuous person avoids the excesses—too much or too little—in order to contribute to the well-being of oneself and the general community. Attempting personal virtue is a microcosm of a society guided by the virtues. A citizen who recognizes the plight of a victim of injustice reflects the society that practices on-going justice. A compassionate neighbor echoes the community's concerns about the less fortunate.

Virtue ethics is additionally concerned with moral pedagogy and possible role models or exemplars. Echoing Plato's plans in *The Republic* and Aristotle's case for the goal of eudomania, supporters of virtue ethics continually debate on how we learn virtues or adopt vices. Music, education, popular entertainment, upstanding institutions all need to be involved in the achievement of a virtuous citizenry or the prevention of corrupting vices. The tales of moral exemplars are central to this undertaking. By telling and retelling their moral lives—from kindergarten tales about Abraham Lincoln or Martin Luther King Jr., to film presentations of Gandhi or Nelson Mandela, the rest of us are introduced to standards or ideals of human conduct.

Lingis is not convinced. He finds numerous counterexamples of what seem to be virtuous acts that bear little resemblance to a harmonious life of moderation that could be a microcosm of a harmonious society. Many of his tales reflect individuals whose courage or sense of justice began with a surprising passion or unexpected imperative. He also finds humans to be a more contrary lot than assumed by supporters of virtue ethics, insofar as there are humans who embody an admirable case of virtue regardless of their habits (or lack of), unusual upbringing or dismal environment. While we can be moved by the persuasive powers of reason, we often are struck by how we can inexplicably be compelled by non-rational forces.

In contrast to the virtue ethics tradition that emphasizes an integral and enduring self, Lingis proposes that the truth of the self is not constant. In part this is due to how passions promise or threaten a transformation in oneself. They alter our sense of space and time, our relation to others and to the world. Lingis does not find this account of passion in mainstream Western philosophy and ethics, but in the great tragedies of the literature and cinema. "Impassioned states are not reactions proportionate to the situation," writes Lingis, "they are excessive...These open the organism to the outside; its senses scan the environment, and the organism moves to take hold of substances and sustenance to satisfy its needs."[9]

This perspective moves Lingis to conclude that whatever virtue status one ascribes to a passion, it cannot be expected to mirror a harmonious society, for an excessive passion attaches itself to "the dense and enigmatic reality of something alien to itself." Here, he discovers moments and deeds of virtue that arise in excessive natures. Individuals act in ways they never believed were possible and in situations so atypical or extraordinary that virtuous habits can neither anticipate nor prepare for them. Hence many of the stories he writes about occur in extreme circumstances, such as rebels holed up against the Nicaraguan government's military thugs, guides traversing the Sahara desert, performance artists in Paris undergoing cosmetic surgery before a live audience, street urchins negotiating the slums of Calcutta, a father in Pennsylvania summoning the nerve to be on the first flight of his son the pilot.

These circumstances are not the stuff of harmonious societies or communities reflecting the virtues of individual citizens. These circumstances are extreme, erratic, oppressive or intensely personal and singular. They spur their own atypical excessive responses and forces. That is one reason Lingis avoids the emphasis on virtues and instead focuses on their excessive resemblances such as visions, imperatives and passions. The laughter of Wayne and Cheryl are central to this focus.

Stories and Arguments

Skeptics of Lingis acknowledge the charm of his style, rhetorical skills, wide-range of sources and lyrical if not mystical presentation of descriptions and personal accounts. But they find no effort in establishing an argument. They cannot find signs of deductive or inductive reasoning that show how premises support a particular conclusion or present a sustained objection to another argument.

Underlying the dramatic accounts of Wayne and Cheryl is a logical strain in Lingis's thought that actually is quite classical in presentation. It relies on empirical facts while addressing the assumptions or implications of those facts. There is an initial thesis: harmonious society spawns virtuous individuals, while such individuals contribute to a more harmonious community and society. This thesis is supported by the significance of moral exemplars who have been esteemed as role models for the rest of the citizenry. It is also supported by observing those chaotic societies where the virtues have been abandoned or corrupted. The more virtuous the community or society, the more civil and human we become.

Lingis's account of Wayne and Cheryl's story is only one of his many counterexamples to the initial thesis. They question the notion that ostensibly beacons of harmonious society — business corruptions, military miscues, academic foibles — that highlight shortcomings and superficialities of so-called virtuous institutions. This is an initial premise in Lingis's argument. The major and positive premise is that Lingis's examples are more than anecdotal evidence or fuel to flame the fires attacking modernity. The major premise is more affirmative. It sees Wayne and Cheryl as one of so many sample cases found in Lingis's writings that eventually confirm a plausible and general conclusion. At the risk of simplifying this conclusion, we can call it an Alternate Thesis insofar as it recognizes the centrality of passions in the experiences of other communities. These passions are more than expressions of an emotion or feeling. They are also a form of knowledge.

Students of philosophy often consider whether the certainty of knowledge is based on eternal forms, deductive proofs or justified true beliefs. When presented with controversies over abortion or altruistic killings, they deal with far-fetched examples such as a famous violinist finding himself in a hospital room hooked up to a blood transfusion machine or a pedestrian suddenly confronted with a falling trolley car and not sure whether to sacrifice an innocent bystander in order to save the trolley's passengers.

Lingis's arguments for the intricate relation between passions and knowledge are based on the lived stories of others. The certainty of this knowledge that generates his subsequent reflections is found in the faces, bodies and voices of those who tell and retell their stories. He does not deny that there are important truths that emerge from the rational community. He does affirm truths that illuminate other communities in which the force of passions becomes fundamental. In the case of Wayne and Cheryl, among so many others, Lingis discovers an ephemeral and intense community of courage, love and laughter.

Notes

1. Friedrich Nietzsche, *The Gay Science,* trans. Walter Kaufmann (New York: Vintage, 1974), #324.
2. Lingis, *Trust,* 109-126.
3. Lingis, *The First Person Singular,* 75.
4. Lingis, *Trust,* 126.
5. Anca Parvulescu, *Laughter: Notes on a Passion* (Cambridge, MA: MIT Press, 2010).
6. Georges Bataille, *Inner Experience,* trans. Leslie Anne Boldt (Albany, NY: State University Press of New York, 1988), 95-96.
7. Parvulescu, *Laughter,* 89.
8. Lingis, *Trust,*118.

9. Alphonso Lingis, "Aconcagua", in *Passion in Philosophy*, ed. Randolph C. Wheeler (Lanham: Lexington Books, 2017), 9. For an intriguing historical account of the passions, self-knowledge, moral development in relation to the humors, medical knowledge and developing character, see Noga Arikha, *Passions and Tempers: A History of the Humours* (New York: HarperCollins, 2007). For an informative and thoughtful discussion of the significance of excess from Lingis's perspective in relation to Merleau-Ponty, Heidegger and other central figures in phenomenological tradition, see Tom Sparrow, "Excess in Existence", in *Passion in Philosophy*, 17-26.

Chapter Six

Pet Subjects: Strangers, Dogs and Beggars

In the sweltering 90-degree heat of downtown Baltimore, a frail man stands by a bustling intersection waiting for the light to change to red. The scribbled sign in his hand—stating he's homeless, unemployed, recovering addict, forgotten veteran— invites drivers to open their windows and hand him loose change or a bill. So seldom do they bother, the man's task seems hopeless.

Hours later, as the temperature nears three digits, I take the dog for a stroll to a nearby park, where scores of spectators are enjoying a semi-professional women's tennis tournament. The mutt wearily sits under a tree after slurping up water from the ice-filled bottle I dutifully carry for him. Hardly a point ends before strangers approach to ask if they can bring water, a snack or a cup of ice. Not for me, of course, but for the dog.

As we lingered at the tournament, the canine was soon invited by spectators to a smorgasbord of refreshing liquids, leftovers of barbecued chicken, a gentle massage from a fellow dog owner, even a smooch from one of those odd souls who dote on any cuddly beast.

Like a functionary, I answer the typical queries about the dog's breed, age, alpha status and personality. "He's a mix (imagine a husky mounting a beagle, speculated one canine aficionado), the pound said about 10 months old, friendly and hasn't bitten anyone (yet), playful but doesn't much listen (just like my children), and yes, he's been fixed." Such questions are not directed to me. There is no curiosity about my family heritage, dietary habits or procreative capacities.

Later at the intersection, another beggar tries his luck. No one strokes the back of his neck, offers him tasty treats, rubs his belly or hands him a cold drink. At most, he'll sporadically take loose change from begrudging or guilt-ridden drivers who hastily roll up their windows before he gets to mutter thanks, God bless or good day. For him, unlike the dog, there will be no sloppy kiss from a complete stranger.

Important Creatures

Much of Lingis's thought is devoted to the multifarious encounters with strangers. So many times we simply ignore them or they neglect us, be it in foreign lands or among everyday neighbors. But the stories that make up our lives often derive from these encounters. The stories we tell one another are rarely restatements of a narrative. Each time I tell my mundane tale about taking Sparky to a nearby tennis tournament, some details I embellish, others are deleted and, depending on the audience, I'll wait to see how they start telling stories about their dogs, those in their childhood and those who might be their current companions.

Although primary attention to these encounters has been on the human-to-human, Lingis often writes about the human encounter with nature and its non-human creatures. For many of his readers, this encounter arises not in jungles where predatory beasts might be prowling, but through our relation with formerly wild animals that have become domesticated.[1] Although his essays devote considerable attention to mythical, nomadic, sacred, monumental accounts of the relation between humans and animals, he says very little about the most frequent or endearing contacts his readers mostly likely have with animals — as pets. Yet his ideas on communication, trust, accompaniment and subjectivity shed considerable light on the ambivalent lives of animals as pets.

In the following pages we rely on Lingis's perspectives on philosophical story-telling as a venue to describe the lives of pets, particularly dogs, and their uneven relationships with owners (or guardians) and people. Given their ability to smell, hear, chase and protect—not to mention an intelligence that allows them an impressive range of lessons from their human masters, dogs have been recognized as one of the most important animals in human history. Pedestrians and passersby warm up to strange dogs more easily than unfamiliar human beings. Want to gain an insight to neighbors or newcomers? Ask about their dogs. They can cheerfully and willingly tell you more stories about their dogs than about their family, workplace or ex-lovers. Telling stories about the dog is, after all, in part telling a story about themselves.

Pets

A pet is an animal with a name, welcomed to one's humble abode, and whose mortality deserves a respect not given to insects annihilated by a can of Raid or chickens doomed in abattoirs. A pet descends from a feral creature who is now allowed to reside near or within the domestic quarters of its owners. In becoming a pet, though, the animal forfeits some of its basic urges, such as hunting, procreating, wandering and playing with the herd or pack. The wolf that sacrifices these urges eventually becomes the dog that herds rather than kills the sheep, who retrieves the fallen bird to its owner rather than gobbling the fresh catch for himself. This wolf also becomes the dog that is now seemingly satisfied fetching a stick in the back yard.

In this transformation, humans have discovered that pets, especially dogs, can be companions or friends, if not members of the family. The show poodle, the sled-pulling Siberian huskie, the drug-sniffing hound, the shepherd leading a blind person, or the fierce Rottweiler protecting the castle or urban backyard are only some of the purposes offered by dogs. There is truth to the axiom about a dog being a man's best friend, except it also extends to women, people of all ages and numerous cultures.

There is considerable dispute over whether a dog is a true

pet if it is being exploited by its owner. Fighting dogs reflect the masculine and commercial ambitions of their owners and are lucky to reach middle age. Male show dogs are expected to show two symmetrical testicles. One owner of an apparent mono-testicular show dog quickly found a cosmetic surgeon to implant a second testicle. (Alas, during one competition the second natural testicle dropped into the scrotum, thus turning the dog into a three-testicle freak.) For fear of a facial scar or even a minor physical injury, show dogs do not go to local parks to play and wrestle with other dogs.

At times one hears of drastic measures taken by owners to hold on to their beloved mutt. Sick and dying pets often receive considerable and expensive attention, such as hip replacement or chemotherapy, from their owners or guardians, even if the 16-year-old canine (over 100 in human years) is clearly miserable. Indeed, with pet cloning possibilities emerging, veteran journalist John Woestendiek reports that one owner paid a DNA procurer $150,000 for a copy of her tamed bull Chance who, when cloned, would be named Second Chance.[2] Another owner, wanting a genetic sample of her dying dog, had a rod shoved through his rectum to the abdomen to retrieve a reliable biopsy for possible cloning. The pain inflicted upon the suffering animal seems an afterthought to the owner fearful of facing the future without her Booger. Such anecdotes force us to consider what counts as a real pet and a true owner.

The stories told by dog owners admit some of the excessive harms done by selfish owners. But these are exceptions and should not overshadow the distinct joys brought by these animals. For them their experiences with a dog is not an object for their interests, but another subject who reflects, emotes, senses and communicates. Dogs and owners have a special connection. In more ways than one these creatures from the distant wild have become pet subjects.

Canine Camaraderie

Levinas never really addressed the issue of other species. He would say that the difference between a dog that faces me and my child who faces me is that when I respond to the needs of a child, they are unending whereas the dog's needs are limited and finite. But I don't see that this is an essential difference.

Lingis[3]

Most any dog owner would concur. For them it is the dog above all other creatures who illuminates and embodies fundamental virtues. We can only wish humans could be so strong. Canine virtues such as loyalty, courage and unconditional love are legendary. As any dog owner gladly attests, you can wake in the morning feeling and looking a mess, so much so that the grouchy boyfriend or demanding girlfriend doesn't want to touch you until lunchtime. But the pooch is different—it can be eight in the morning and the mutt still offers you a sloppy kiss, with tail wagging, delighted to see you just as you are.

As with most domestic animals, dogs have often been bred for specific human purposes. The various types of shepherd assist humans to keep watch over sheep or cattle; the St Bernard carries a flask of booze for the mountaineer, retrievers retrieve the bounties of hunters and terriers terrorize earthly prey by digging into the grounds to fetch a meal for their owners. Even the current terrier strain gone bad—the notorious pit bull—is designed to produce gambling profits and bragging rights for its owner.

Such cases show that we are uneven when it comes to seeing canine comrades as objects for our human well-being or subjects in a primarily human world.

Dog Parks

In a gesture of gratitude, affection and convenience, humans have turned numerous locales into dog parks. Nestled in urban settings, they elude official designation. That is, a pedestrian generally does not see a sign proclaiming the park as a place for dogs to run about and play with one another. In most cities it is illegal to unleash a dog in public. Bypassing civic ordinances, dog park visitors are guided by unwritten principles or codes of conduct which, in contrast to corporate structures or institutions, are fairly minimal. Briefly: control your dog, and quickly but safely intervene upon the start of excessive growling, biting or humping. And always clean up your dog's mess.

Predictably, even these minimal rules are unevenly interpreted. After all, they pertain to descendants of wolves running free amid an urban populace. Though pets are brought to the park to play and mingle, consensus on canine sociability is unclear. Growling can be interpreted as anger, but after the dogs are separated they usually wag their tails and rejoin the tumble. Biting seems violent, but when dogs go jowl to jowl or lay their teeth on each other's ears, how do we know they are not doing their seductive version of a French kiss or a sensual nibble on the lobe?

As within human circles, perspectives on canine humping are quite ambiguous. While the tendency to hump spans breeds and ages, the most problematic humper in the park is usually the unneutered male dog. Wanton in selecting a mate, he stirs trouble among the other dogs. Like Christians who momentarily forgot about God while attending a Roman spectacle, the virile dog seems temporarily oblivious to his master's commands to dismount. Occasionally male owners strut beside their four-legged stud and explain how their pet's lack of discipline can be attributed to the principle of all strong alpha males—assert dominance, implying that sex is a secondary issue. Female owners invariably chortle over these accounts, observing that indiscriminate humping is a male trait across all species.

Initial encounters at the park are fairly simple. Owners first acknowledge one another by trading the names, ages and origins of their pets. Curiously, people have an easier time remembering these details than the names of owners. Should they bump into each other at the neighborhood store, they look, pause, then note, "Oh, you are Reuben's owner."

Perhaps visitors readily remember the various names because they realize that names for dogs are not mere appendages. Echoing Medievalist thought, pet names tend to designate their very being. Dogs given childlike names as Taylor, Arnie or Percy easily heed the parental calls. "This is not how you play with other dogs"; or, "Stop, that is inappropriate behavior." Those bearing musical monikers, such as Elvis, Jazz, Casey (Jones), Bono (of U2), Abbey (Road), more easily harmonize with the other dogs. Ginseng and Ginger add spice to their owners' lives. Blazer really does blaze gracefully across the fields, Sparky can spark up the playful energies of fellow mutts, and Saint acts saintly with the puppies and children who frolic nearby.

Admittedly, among dogs named after immortal and demonic powers, such as Zeus or Caesar, there is greater reluctance to heed the cries of their mortal guardians. What do they care about inappropriate behavior? Indeed, dogs named after Nero, Odin, Rex or Thor, thump, dump and hump wherever and whenever they damn well please!

Communication and Intimate Zones

In closing "What is Passed Over in Communication", Lingis asserts that, "Sometimes one finds then that, like the one that opens his house to a passerby and speaks meaningless conventions without query or truth, one's voice is a murmur that delineates and condenses a zone of intimacy and hospitality."[4]

Veterinarian and scholar James Serpell cautions against overstating the endless quirks told and retold about humans and their pets. For these quirks have always been among pet owners, only now the rapid increase of pet keeping increasingly carries a vestige of the eccentricities of royalty and millionaires who could first afford a menagerie of beasts and the servants to care for them. Serpell acknowledges the elaborate attention of owners who provide air conditioning for the doghouse, adorn the pet with boutique clothing, or purchase special grooming services and cosmetic make-overs. More typical are the cases where people welcome into their home a variety of animals whose ancestors were predators, scavengers and pack animals who ruled the wilderness.

In their dogs, humans find a semblance of natural forces tempered by breeding, cultivation and domestication. Regardless of lingering feral characteristics, having a dog is an opportunity for humans to find in other animals a friend, confidante or companion. To skeptics who regard pets as symbolic substitutes for more fulfilling human contacts, Serpell contends that animal companions offer an enriching feature of life. Comparable to marriage, friendship or the parent-child relation, he claims, pet ownership offers an assortment of trusting and reliable companionships; it even "can indeed have a measurable impact on human susceptibility to physical and mental disease."[5] For many humans the most authentic communication and intimate honesty is found with domestic animals rather than fellow humans.

Dog parks and pets in general offer the chance for humans to reorient themselves with a relation to an aspect of nature, though not an entirely wild aspect. If there is any obstacle to animal/human communication, it lies not with the pet's lack of language but human hubris. Annabelle Sabloff argues that this hubris in part lies with our exaggerated focus on language. Our linguistic conventions and metaphors need drastic revision. The humane is good and bestial is bad distinction, for instance, should be replaced with terms that highlight the continuities between animals and humans.

In place of the muted relation urban and suburban residents

have had with animals, Sabloff recommends more enriching forms of communication. Dogs seem to have more to say than any other non-human mammal. From the mouth that barks, howls or growls to the tail that wags or droops, the dog, according to Desmond Morris[6], conveys a variety of messages to humans, other animals and fellow canines. Best-selling dog writer Elizabeth Thomas[7] speculates that the obstacle to proper communication is human stubbornness. The source of knowledge about species stems not so much from a human vantage point but from an intuition or empathy received from non-human animals. Forget about anthropomorphism, she advises, and support caninomorphism.

That animals can be equal (even superior) partners in communication is evident in prudential matters. Female owners swear their dogs are gifted jerk detectors, having an uncanny sense to know quickly whether a prospective beau is worthy. Barking at the newcomer as he first enters the front door is not a cute expression of jealousy, but rather a confidential warning: dump this guy, now.

One regular at the dog park made some extra money taking care of pets while the owners took a short vacation. She stopped by the evening before the departure for directions. When it comes to parents of toddlers, baby-sitters are given their cell phone numbers and the pediatrician's emergency number. When it comes to dog-sitters, there can be two pages of instructions. Reviewing the details, the dog-sitter asked the owners if they shut their suitcases. No, they replied, why should we? Because, replied the sitter, your dog knows you are leaving for an extended weekend, might be jealous, and will pee on your clothes in the suitcase. Immediately the owners checked. Sure enough, their clothes were drenched.

Undoubtedly miscommunication also arises. For example, the owner of Wilbur, named in honor of the renowned pig, reports walking his dog along the sidewalk when a black Lab was approaching with a female owner. Recalling the recent scuffle Wilbur had with a similar Lab several days before, the owner sensed possible trouble and began crossing the street. The Lab's owner noticed the detour and called out that her dog likes to play. Wilbur's owner, long a stutterer, was caught by surprise and muttered a hurried but misspoken rejoinder. "S-s-sorry, my dog has a p-p-problem with black dogs." The woman then hurried over to impose a 10-minute lecture to Wilbur's owner on the wrongs of raising a racist dog.

Sunshine

The touch of the other, the touch of a mortal alterity is a contact, a contagion, and not a communication of information or of understanding; it is the transmission of a trembling on the limits of beings.
Lingis[8]

Summer holiday in Baltimore, another muggy evening, and there is only one animal emergency hospital taking new patients. The waiting room is a bit sparse. A couple of cats with possible infections, a 12-year-old Golden Retriever troubled by adverse reactions to chemotherapy, a wild goose coughing incessantly from a damaged throat, and some clients trying to take their recovering patients back home.

Then a woman, barely 5 feet tall, somewhat burly with strands of frazzled gray hair, carries a panting dog through the front door. Sunshine seems almost as big as she. His eyes, at least the parts not covered by straggling and matted hair, are glazed over. He is shivering and drooling. Minutes after arriving, Sunshine pees on the floor. Oblivious to the surroundings and so pathetic is his pose that neither the cats bother to hiss nor dogs growl. Everyone suspects Sunshine is dying.

His owner is not convinced. She cradles Sunshine, assuring

him with incantations that "Mama's here, Mama's here." With a moment's break, she looks around and asks about the other animals. She learns that the cats have allergies, the retriever's cancer might be in remission, the blue-eyed dog needed only a couple of stitches, and the wild goose was found in a pond by a woman who cannot bear to see any animal suffer. Quickly her attention is again absorbed with Sunshine's palpitations, more urination on the floor, and his unwillingness to drink water.

She refuses to believe the evidence. Though Sunshine is only 3 years old, he has never been healthy. She discovered him because his fur and skin were so foul that the owners found him repulsive. Besides the stench, his infections posed a health risk to the neighboring children. In impoverished West Virginia, where even healthy pets have trouble finding stable homes, Sunshine was a day from death's door.

To gain a reprieve, the whims of fortune for once went his way. By chance Sunshine's next owner, the one caring for him in this emergency room, had to spot his plight on an internet rescue site and travel 300 miles at a moment's notice. She bypassed numerous shelters on the way, ignoring the whimpers and barks emanating from the regional rescue organizations and adoption agencies which could have shortened her trip. Only this mangy, flea infested, rotten smelling mongrel, with a congenital heart condition, was destined for her. The seizure that brought these two to the emergency room likely stems from this malformed heart. Unprepared for the Baltimore heat and smog, Sunshine is again at death's door.

Stroking Sunshine's neck, she assures him there will be another tomorrow. When he calms down for a couple of minutes, she cheerfully engages others in the waiting room with anecdotes about friends and acquaintances who build aquariums or aviaries so that their exotic fish or birds can display their beauty. Fellow animal guardians join in and recall how a retired couple is simply mesmerized by a tank full of nearly extinct salt-water fish and how neighbors took in feline and canine strays. Sunshine's owner lightens the somber mood by focusing on pet subjects. It gets fellow owners to forget their own animal's plight and smile again.

They, like Sunshine's owner, are not dolts. They are cognizant of possible complications in their pets' medical treatments; they realize the risks taken when bringing these unwanted or endangered creatures into their own homes. They shrug their shoulders on any discussion about rational interests and long-range social benefits. The silence that intersperses these moments is a shared recognition among the owners that their being in this emergency room is an expenditure without recompense.

This recognition evokes an unbounded happiness that Friedrich Nietzsche envisioned as a humaneness of the future. This humaneness, he writes, is exemplified in the "happiness of a god full of power and love, full of tears and laughter, a happiness that, like the sun in the evening, continually bestows its inexhaustible riches, pouring them into the sea, feeling richest, as the sun does, only when even the poorest fisherman is still rowing with golden oars!"[9]

In silence this frazzled woman pours her inexhaustible riches on a singular creature, Sunshine. There can be no rational—biological, utilitarian, social reciprocity—justification behind her act. To raise the issue about interests, rights or proportionality is pointless. She is acting out of a happiness in which her divine powers are surprisingly discovered.

Natural Goodness?

As my daughter and I, with stitched-up mutt in the back seat, leave the emergency center, we reach a stoplight with another beggar shuffling in the stifling heat. Waiting for the light to turn green, we recall the animal hospital's television reporting how progressive cities such as San Francisco are enacting policies to eliminate panhandlers. And we recall San Francisco to be the same city that boasts of building modern temporary shelters for stray animals, including air conditioning, bathing, attentive volunteers and furniture plusher than what millions of the world's impoverished children have.

As in other cities, officials in Baltimore alert us to how these pesky strangers—beggars, not other animals—are so prevalent. Even my 12-year-old daughter can recite the rationales for neglecting them: the beggar will take the money to buy some drugs or cheap booze; or, given his healthy appearance, it is just a ruse for us to reward his slothful ways.

Such rationales are lacking when it comes to the stray cat or dog, the wounded bird or squirrel. We do not speculate whether the wandering mutt was exiled because the pack found him driven by gluttony or lust. Whatever potential dangers, a prospective human owner can readily have them neutered, declawed, medicated or caged. The reasons for being abandoned are negligible, for the animal is presumed innocent. We look into those soft and vulnerable canine eyes and see only natural goodness.

This courtesy of presumed innocence and natural goodness is not extended to the beggar standing in the sweltering heat, his eyes making a quick check to see if we might be tossing money his way. We assure ourselves that we know the vices bringing him here. Tugging on the thoughts of an owner who just spent a week's pay for the dog's hip replacement or chemotherapy must be some wish to engage in a momentary exchange with the beggar. Do you have a family? How long have you been doing this? Where do you go when it is cold and rainy?

Yet no word suffices for the destitute. Perhaps they too await a god who possesses the powers of the sun. Not so they can pocket a couple of quarters to buy a cup of coffee, a bowl of warm soup or some cheap wine, but so they can depart with golden oars and never return. They await the tenderness and good cheer of a big-hearted woman and her Sunshine.

Notes

1. Lingis, *The First Person Singular*, 31-35.
2. John Woestendiek, *Dog, Inc.: How a Collection of Visionaries, Rebels, Eccentrics and Their Pets Launched the Commercial Dog Cloning Industry* (New York: Penguin, 2102).
3. Randolph C. Wheeler, "Alterity after Infinity: Interview with Alphonso Lingis", in *Passion in Philosophy*, 95.
4. Lingis, *Sensation*, 96.
5. James Serpell, *In The Company of Animals* (Cambridge: Cambridge University Press, 1997).
6. Desmond Morris, *Dogwatching* (New York: Crown, 1986) and Annabelle Sabloff, *Reordering the World: Humans and Animals in the City* (Toronto: University of Toronto Press, 2001). Curiously, while there is considerable discussion about the essential relation between the human and the lived body—sexed or gendered, assertive or empowered, healthy or mobile—there is much less attention to the bodies of pets and how they are radically altered by being domesticated, including their ears being cropped, claws eliminated, genitals removed, among other things.
7. Elizabeth Thomas, *The Social Lives of Dogs* (New York: Pocket Books, 2000). For a moving and insightful account of having a wolf as a pet, see Mark Rowlands, *The Philosopher and the Wolf: Lessons from the Wild on Love, Death, and Happiness* (New York: Pegasus Books, 2009).
8. Lingis, *Deathbound Subjectivity*, 189.
9. Nietzsche, *The Gay Science*, #337.

Part 2

Existential Genealogy

Chapter Seven

Genealogy as Philosophy

I take the opportunity provided by this treatise to express publicly and formally a desire I have previously voiced only in occasional conversation with scholars; namely, that some philosophical faculty might advance historical *studies of* morality *through a series of academic prize essays—perhaps this book will serve to provide a powerful impetus in this direction.*
Nietzsche[1]

Introduction

This chapter attempts the following. It outlines how genealogy has become a distinct philosophical inquiry as initiated by Nietzsche. One direction influenced by this inquiry is found in the work of Michel Foucault. He deploys a two-pronged approach—archaeology and genealogy—to philosophical investigations. Notwithstanding the remarkable research spawned by Foucault's ideas, it neglects any sustained attention to the experiences and reflections of those whose lives are being highlighted in genealogy's research and critique into the birth, and possible death, of human ideals.

How to address this neglect is found in many of Lingis's writings. He also emphasizes attention to aspects of change, break, rupture, transgression. His focus, however, is often centered on an experience other thinkers give scant attention to—namely, the moments of when or how a break was to be brought about by human beings in unique circumstances. These can be intense, comical, disturbing, curious, impassioned or daring. Lingis's photographic attention to the faces of others, and his colorful and dramatic portrayals of individuals and communities from all corners of the planet, guide his studies of the circumstances and drama of their anticipation and actions for a different tomorrow. We call this direction existential genealogy.

Giorgio Agamben claims genealogy introduces a new paradigm or conceptual lens as a way of organizing and understanding facts, ideas and experiences.[2] It also constantly questions or examines our own relation to this paradigm, with the possible paradox that genealogy highlights the goal of examining human ideals without possible realization of that goal, and how that realization is caught between reconciling the past with the present. Agamben's analysis of historical signatures is indebted to Foucault's genealogical paradigm, while recognizing its paradoxical trait of demonstrating the emergence of a phenomenon without the assurance of duplicating it.

We propose that Lingis's study of the moments when humans act introduces another genealogical paradigm. It too evokes a potential paradox. It studies the committed act of those who dare to anticipate a different tomorrow or near future, but neither the reader nor Lingis, nor those who dare, will likely be sure what has emerged from the act.

As developed by Nietzsche, genealogy addresses conventional themes—truth, justice, beauty, self-knowledge, human ideals—through a different conceptual lens. Genealogy focuses on how their cultural or moral influences or effects began, prevailed or lost intellectual potency. Genealogy addresses intellectual disputes not only in terms of a possible standard of independent objectivity. Nietzsche proposes his genealogy as a scholarly basis or theory school for subsequent research. It aims to study potential effects, successes or dangers, if or when a particular ideal emerges and takes hold. Amid these proposals Nietzsche outlines three methodological tasks to pursue this inquiry.

Three Tasks

While many philosophers have addressed historical issues in

relation to studying morality, Nietzsche's genealogy is distinct in that it focuses on the origins of a morality in order to examine its effectiveness, truthfulness and authority. In his view this study must also address the conditions and circumstances behind the emergence or birth of a moral belief or principle.

Given Nietzsche's inimical penchant for hyperbole, he proposes his genealogy to be an analysis of the value of values that might be uncannier than any previous analysis.[3] As highlighted in his quasi-autobiographical work *Ecce Homo*, Nietzsche sees his *Genealogy* as a play of calculations that gradually becomes an intense moment of learning a new truth. He then asserts that the three essays comprising the *Genealogy* are distinct inquiries—first into the truth of the birth of Christianity and the spirit of *ressentiment*, second into the birth of conscience and its reliance on the human use of cruelty, and third into the triumph of the ascetic ideal as presented to generations of believers or practitioners of some variants of asceticism.

The range and scope of proposals and contentions in Nietzsche's genealogy has spawned a variety of directions for philosophical inquiry. There is genealogy as polemic that confronts and wages an intellectual battle with influential ideals or conventional values. By depicting their origins genealogy shows that these ideals are not anchored by established truths but rather by favorable conditions that have their own tenuous legacy. There is genealogy that undermines perennial moral values such as pity, altruism, equality and those who embody or promote them—the priest, servant, even parent, professional or educator. The efforts to promote altruism or self-sacrifice could be psychological maneuvers to have people esteem their own suffering in the name of goodness.

There is also an on-going debate over whether Nietzsche's use of genealogy is to describe and analyze the birth or replacement of a value or ideal in order to directly or indirectly promote an alternative normative code of ethics. This debate focuses on

Nietzsche's flourishing language and accounts of humans as herd animals, masters and slaves, sick and healthy, rancorous or honest in order to decide whether Nietzsche actually ranked humans in terms of strength and weakness, creative and reactive, pitiful or noble.

These takes on genealogy tend to approach Nietzsche as an antagonist of a distant opponent who is either a historical relic or an easy target that gained popular approval and needs to be exposed. While the rhetoric and analyses of the ascetic priest or *ressentiment* bear elements of sarcasm and vitriol, the initial concern is not about a third party. We are reminded of Nietzsche's claim that his initial focus is on the origin of "our moral prejudices."[4] It is not just the moral preachings and practices of others that concern the genealogical impetus. It is our own beliefs—whether genuine or feeble, informed or imaginary, cheerful or rancorous, the fruit of love or law—that first draws his philosophical scrutiny.

The first sentence of the *Genealogy* states, "We are unknown to ourselves, we men of knowledge—and with good reason." Yet the first sentence of the very next passage sets out to examine the ideals of a man who is a bit of mystery to himself. This paradoxical plight—how can one come to know the world but not oneself?—fuels many of Nietzsche's subsequent observations about the value of values, starting with Socrates' esteem of the dictum "Know Thyself" to the current ideals that amount to little more than "our moral prejudices."

The term "our" might have several references. It could allude to Nietzsche and his small circle of friends or readers. "Our moral prejudices" also invokes the notion that we have abided by or endorsed values and ideals that have an enduring tradition or remarkable effectiveness. Nietzsche could be playful with the first person plural, often claiming that he is part of and outside those he critiques. In any event, the Preface is not accusatory. It rarely mentions "you" except as a possible reader. Nietzsche's genealogy has us as a starting point. To examine our moral prejudices Nietzsche outlines three tasks that comprise his genealogy as a philosophical enterprise.

First is the task to raise novel questions and see through new eyes what Nietzsche calls the "hidden land of morality." This hidden land harbors not only the thoughts of some obscure scholars and influential persons. For Nietzsche the hidden land refers to "...morality that has actually existed, actually been lived..."[5] The ostensible values of pity or *ressentiment* are more than intellectual debates for genealogy — it must also discern what it means to live or relate to other humans via pity or *ressentiment*. Nietzsche's extended quote from Tertullian about laughing over those pagans who are descending into eternal damnation is quite telling of a life full of rancor. The litany of harsh punishments in the name of progress, humanity, enlightenment or faith show components of a moral life where so many good things rely on cruelty.

Confirmation is the second task. Genealogy's favorite color, says Nietzsche, is gray. Only that which can be documented and proven to have happened interests the inquiry into the history of a moral value. Fanciful speculations and imaginary counterexamples such as the trolley dilemma do not pertain. Nietzsche is intrigued by more gripping and existential dilemmas. What does it mean to take on debt and become a creditor? How could someone obligate his or her future to an agreement made — and possibly from guilt or coercion — in the present moment? Does not this obligation require a special faculty of memory and there will be needed special tools and painful techniques to enhance this memory? To address these questions genealogy finds sufficient evidence in human life as found in classic literature or historical materials.

Admittedly, Nietzsche embellishes the task by talking about subterranean venues where moral ideals are manufactured and encounter stench, mendacity and self-abasement. He peers into the workshop where certain moral ideals are manufactured and finds that adherents preach loving one's neighbor while nervously sweating. At the end, though, this philosophical venture has cheerfulness as a possible reward— "in my own language, gay science."[6]

The third methodological task involves engaging other fields of knowledge. In closing the First Essay, Nietzsche pushes for an "amicable and fruitful exchange" among philosophers and those in the fields of medicine, physiology, biology, history, psychology and other diverse perspectives.[7] Regardless of his sardonic observations, Nietzsche incorporates the resources of Darwinists, literary figures, French statesmen, Biblical passages and Early Christian Fathers. To understand the sense of guilt in all of its cunning, philosophy needs the insights of those who can tell us how guilt affects our minds and bodies, its status in the improvement of the species or potential force in altering the direction of personal rancor. Philosophers can learn from other fields how martyrdom can transform its possible witnesses through public spectacle. Historians and sociologists might provide insights into the effect spectacles create and the "orgy of sensations" for those experiencing such moments. In any event, genealogy is a philosophical enterprise that deploys the insights of other disciplines.

Nietzsche is quite direct about these three tasks. In sum, genealogy as philosophy studies how morality is lived, the documentation that supports the different and historical takes on these studies, and the possible contributions from other fields of inquiry in order to grasp the value of our values or the meanings of our ideals. Nietzsche acknowledges that his own inquiry is preparing the stage for subsequent inquiries. He anticipates that his genealogy will be the basis for a school of thought or departure point for further research and taking directions into unexplored areas about the value and meaning of our ideals and practices.

Archaeological Genealogy

One direction is found in the pioneering work of Michel Foucault. His historical genealogies have not only investigated the origins of familiar humanist values or democratic institutions, they have also fostered a variety of research projects that inquire about the status of values and institutions in fields not directly studied by Foucault. For example, his concept of bio-power was formulated in one of his genealogical studies about the birth of modern discipline. It now has sparked its own offshoots for subsequent studies about bio-law, bio-gender or bio-services. His analysis of discipline or sexuality has fueled on-going investigations about how fields of knowledge and forms of power intersect to focus on ordinary experiences and persons.

In his study of the birth of the prison, the asylum or the confession, Foucault abides by the three tasks of Nietzsche's genealogy. He looks to hidden lands of our moral ideals and prejudices, finds how they have been actually lived and practiced while incorporating the research from non-philosophical sources. Foucault's favorite color is also gray, the result of his reliance on printed documents over the centuries since the early Greeks. His hidden lands of where moral ideals thrived feature the lived moralities of obscure figures such as Pierre Riviere, a condemned man subject to public torture, hermaphrodite Herculin Barbin, among many others. Their lives are confirmed in nearly forgotten texts, court records and library archives. Much of Foucault's genealogical studies rely on a variety of sources, including history, political science, criminology, medicine, psychology, biology, among others.

They are archaeological in that Foucault's method relies on documents, established discourses and shifting domains of what counts or does not count as knowledge, and how these shifts intersect with various forms of power, institutional or political. Foucault often begins with an anecdote or scene. Some are comical, others tragic or cruel. They certainly compel a reader's attention. Foucault then traces historical factors that show the introductory story is not simply an anomaly; rather, it emerges from a familiar landscape of modern ideals and humanist values. Much like Nietzsche peering in the workshop where ascetic ideals are made, Foucault gazes into the workshops of humanist ideals to scrutinize their relation to forms of authority, control and efforts to undermine human freedom.

Some critics insist that Foucault presents a dark vision of humanity, one that looks determined or hopeless. Ian Hacking cautions against this interpretation. He claims that Foucault actually studies systems of knowledge and discourse in order to show at what points new ideas or practices were possible (or no longer possible). Ian Hacking underscores this in both his reflections on Foucault and his own genealogical research. "What counts is making a new canvass of possibilities, or rather, restoring one that is now entirely defunct."[8] Hacking adds to this canvass in his own remarkable studies of the mad travelers, child abuse, split personalities or bio-power and statistics.

This "canvass of possibilities" covers considerable territory. One central theme involves the differentiation of times and conditions. Consider Foucault's striking introduction to *Discipline and Punish: The Birth of the Prison*, the only book to be ranked among the 100 most important books of the twentieth century in both philosophy and criminology.[9] The opening chapters present a startling juxtaposition. It begins with the spectacle of an extended torture and public execution that occurs in the late eighteenth century, then abruptly shifts to a meticulous and tedious schedule of a convict's life in a modern prison that becomes typical merely one or two generations later.

What becomes the birth of the prison is not tied to any single date, such as the publication date of the Panopticon in Jeremy Bentham's proposals or the establishment of early penitentiaries in Europe or the United States. The dates are signals or indicators of changing discourses and practices in understanding and addressing crime. Of course, according to Foucault, the modern prison has never diminished crime or made citizens feel more secure. It continues to thrive insofar as its underlying power is manifest in what Foucault calls a disciplinary society. Here techniques of surveillance rather than the brute hand of authority become quite effective with human beings regulating their own behavior while treating everyone else as a potential criminal. In this light, Foucault's history of the present studies a prehistory of conditions and events.

Existential Genealogy

Here we propose a second direction for studying the canvass of possibilities stemming from Nietzsche's enterprise. Based on Lingis's writings we will call this approach existential genealogy. It is presented as a complementary or alternative option rather than an adversary to archaeological genealogy. Admittedly, the term is not found in Lingis's writings and needs some justification.

Many of Lingis's essays sustain the three tasks of Nietzsche's genealogy. His readers discover hidden lands where morality is embodied and practiced in various forms. While Foucault tends to feature intriguing and relatively anonymous figures in Western European history, Lingis presents detailed sketches of lived moralities in remote locales throughout the world, from ancient centers of civilizations to obscure villages and nomadic tribes. They are as anonymous to the reader as the characters introduced by Foucault's genealogical explorations.

Second, Lingis's description of these lives is confirmed in his vivid phenomenological accounts of their actions, words and projects. With his photographs and illuminating portrayals of sundry individuals in their ceremonial clothes, festive parades or sacred rituals, Lingis's accounts offer a colorful patina that complements the scholarly gray favored by Nietzsche and Foucault.

Lingis carries on genealogy's third task with his frequent incorporation of the latest research garnered from other fields. He cites recent findings of cosmologists and physicists as well as the insights and controversies of evolutionists and Freudians. Paleontologists and primatologists inform Lingis's philosophical lens when determining the extent that human beings are extensions of the animal world or an aberration of nature's ways. Should he present the lives of Mongolian nomads who invite him to their homes and wanderings, he includes a historical backdrop of Mongolia's troubled past with its neighbors, the enduring reputation of Genghis Khan, and a detailed sketch of the mountains, climate and natural surroundings that shape their everyday lives. When introducing the life of a vagabond or local urchin, Lingis often provides the context of the political or economic developments that set the moment when a reader encounters these other lives.

Several points distinguish the two. Foucault clearly eschews existential phenomenology as a useful tool for undertaking historical inquiry. In *The Order of Things* and *Archaeology of Knowledge* he specifies its limitations in light of the emphasis on intentionality, intersubjective life-worlds, rational consciousness, and the relation of language to thought. Lingis, always a proponent and practitioner of phenomenology, also has disputes with existentialism. He introduces *Sensation*[10] by arguing against several notable tenets held by existentialist thinkers. The focus on nothingness and negation, whether in relation to being or the relation to others, ignores the positive plenitude and excess found among human beings. The existentialist emphasis on a holistic sense of consciousness and self Lingis finds untenable because it downplays the encounter with another as distinctly different or singular. He suspects existentialists have little regard for the loss or forgetfulness of self that highlights some of the most intense or ecstatic human experiences. And existentialists exaggerate the importance of truth in speech while failing to outline how "authentic responsibility" emerges in communication.

Still, Lingis does not entirely abandon several existential themes. As his photographs and vivid descriptions indicate, the faces and bodies of humans remain central to philosophical reflection. The focus on commitments or projects is frequently animated in Lingis's writings, as well as the sense of absurdity and comical found in various contexts of those projects. And the fascinating details and chance encounters that highlight human ventures which enliven the thoughts of Kierkegaard, Dostoyevski, Nietzsche, de Beauvoir, Sartre are extended to unexpected venues by Lingis. In this light we use "existential" and not "existentialist" to characterize Lingis's genealogical direction.

Lingis's attention to the moment is central. Whereas archaeological genealogy sees someone's story as a departure point to investigate dimensions of our past, Lingis often presents lucid descriptions of other people's present situations in order to understand how they anticipate the future. During interviews Foucault remarked that his reputation as a champion of discontinuity was exaggerated. If anything, he was as much impressed by continuity—traditions or systems of thought—as the occasional ruptures, shifts and transgressions that threatened them. That is why the tension between continuity and its potential ruptures—births or origins of new power/knowledge dynamics—guides the investigations of archaeological genealogy.

Lingis too is intrigued by breaks and discontinuities. But he looks at a case as if we are witnessing individuals in action, with the myriad details of their lives reported through a quasi-journalistic lens that interweaves the mundane with the spectacular. Unlike Foucault, who introduces a case in order to look back, Lingis presents a case to capture how people anticipate what is going to happen or what they are trying to change. In this sense, whereas Foucault quips that his genealogy is a history of the present, Lingis undertakes a prehistory of the future.

Prehistory

In the middle of the second essay of his Genealogy, Nietzsche opens section #9: "Still retaining the criteria of prehistory (this prehistory is in any case present in all ages or may always reappear)..."[11]

The relation between prehistory and origin or birth of a human ideal is not simply a matter of before and after. Nietzsche's sketches of a prehistory rarely bother with years or dates. When he speculates on the origins of justice, poetry, logic or concept of knowledge he considers the possible functions and effects, conditions that prepared for its beginning, how an ideal could have triumphed and the stakes of the struggle, as well as which adversary or predecessor was displaced or erased.

In consecutive sections of *The Gay Science*, for example, Nietzsche sketches the origins of knowledge and logic. He traces possible links between self-deception, the utility of knowledge and the struggle for knowledge. At first, he speculates that this struggle for knowledge was mostly the different expressions of "an intellectual play impulse, and honesty and skepticism were innocent and happy like all play." Then the pursuit of knowledge began to be taken seriously. Which forms of knowledge were truth or misleading, powerful or weak, signs of conviction or insincerity, become a central concern.

The origin of knowledge begins when innocent play of ideas gives way to something much more serious. In Nietzsche's words, "the intellectual fight became an occupation, an attraction, a profession, a duty, something dignified—and eventually knowledge and the striving for the true found their place as a need among other needs."[12] This need for true knowledge to underscore contemporary disputes and political battles is a startling shift. The philosophical problem Nietzsche concludes is "To what extent truth can endure incorporation? That is the question; that is the experiment."

He follows this remark with another proposal. Humans were not always driven by the rules of reason and basics of logic. There must have been a time when they were guided or propelled by allegedly illogical sources, be they divine or mysterious, derived from royal authority or ancestral ghosts. Two components of being logical include the notion of equality and the concept of substance. Nietzsche does not give examples here, such as "not both A and B" is equivalent to "either not A or not B," or "unmarried adult male is interchangeable with bachelor." He addresses how using logic enhances a group's chances of survival or possible dominance over another group. Logic helps us make judgments, assess accuracy and error, infer new facts from familiar ones. The origin of the of value logic, like the origin of knowledge, lies in its becoming a need as central to human life as water, air and fire.

Prehistory gives more attention to the conditions or background that shapes the emergence of a value or ideal. For example, in his lecture series *Wrong-Doing and Truth-Telling*, Foucault looks into the functions and historical values of the confession. What does it mean to tell the truth about oneself? How does one show to others that we know who we are or what we have done? Foucault analyses the status of confession (or avowal) in the time of the ancient Greeks, how it emerged as a spiritual test among early Christians, and the eventual extent that it was useful in determining the innocence or guilt of a suspected wrong-doer. He takes the reader through an array of practices and rituals that dot the historical landscape.

After Socrates's dictum about "Know Thyself", Foucault traces a variety of attempts to abide by this. One strain was to find a mentor or master who taught the techniques of self-knowledge. The Early Christian Fathers tied the confession to one's sincere relation to Jesus's mission or belief in God. And there were always some conjurers willing to help with knowing oneself by interpreting our dreams, fears or lingering memories.

While the confession was always a part of legal proceedings, gradually it took on a new life. Suspected criminals were no longer expected to at least acknowledge being the author of the crime, but to explain their motives, their plans for escape, the circumstances of their background and relation to the victims. Why all this fuss about the criminal's self-understanding? By the 1800s, according to Foucault, criminal justice needed to distinguish between a mad and a rational criminal, particularly in cases of senseless murder. To make such a distinction, the courts and legal experts needed the criminals to talk about themselves, what was going on in their minds or souls that led them to commit such horrendous deeds. This concern about "homicidal monomania," says Foucault, is the "key notion in the proto-history of criminal subjectivity."[13]

To support this sense of a proto-history, Foucault looks into some horrifying crimes committed during the nineteenth century in Western Europe. There is a man's assault and murder of a young girl. Another young man slaughtered most of his own family. A mother strangled her infant child, but there was legal dispute about whether it was an act of madness or practicality, since the mother was very poor and needed something to feed the rest of the family.

In earlier judicial practices, the conviction and punishment of the alleged miscreant would not need a close review of his or her own words. Determining the veracity and credibility of the miscreant's own words soon became an integral part of the judicial process. They required the expertise of emerging sciences, such as psychology and criminology. While Foucault provides dates, mostly he scrutinizes the conditions and arguments that eventually led to, what he calls, a history of the present.[14]

Criminal subjectivity—the notion that suspected and actual criminals must give some account of themselves, explain their feelings and drives—has become and remains a central theme in modern criminal justice. When sensational trials reach a public audience invariably people want an account from the accused— not just an apology or recognition of the pain the evil deed did, but an account in his own words about his motives, purposes, emotions, thoughts, childhood, social life, why these particular targets or no plans to escape. Does the accused wish to get attention, get even, carry out a command, look into the eyes of survivors of the victims? In these conditions the confession is born. Or, in Foucault's accounts, the confession is reborn in new forms.

For Foucault, these new forms were rendered as births and origins. This is consistent with many of Nietzsche's own titles to his essays and epigraphs, where the origin is a frequent invitation to speculate how an ideal and value was formulated, developed or triumphed. The birth of "criminal subjectivity" is Foucault's way of reminding us that this idea has now become an essential part of contemporary life, from television talk shows to proceedings in criminal justice.

According to Giorgio Agamben, the term "origin" is misplaced and misunderstood when seeing genealogy as another kind of philosophy. For him origin is too limited to chronology or a precise date, a before and after. He prefers displacing origin with more gradual movements, what he calls moments of arising. Agamben's inspiration for this approach is Franz Overbeck, a scholar and good friend of Nietzsche's. Overbeck raises the problem of identifying any inherent correlation between the past, present and future. Agamben quotes Overbeck: "It is only when starting from the essential difference between prehistory and history that one can explain why prehistory enjoys such a special consideration."[15]

Most of us learn history as a series of traditions that lead up to a current and familiar world. Patterns of cause and effect or the clashes of competing traditions become the primary focal points. Not so. The similarities are apparent only after the fact. Overbeck emphasizes the logical awkwardness in identifying a specific point of birth. Moreover, much of the excitement about human beings is actually found in these prehistorical moments. The practice of historical inquiry, contends Agamben, "...must sooner or later engage the constitutive heterogeneity in his or her work."[16]

This heterogeneity applies to Lingis's genealogy, with a twist on time, truth and subjectivity. *Deathbound Subjectivity* opens with a chapter "The Origin of Infinity."[17] There he reviews central thoughts of major figures in the existentialist/phenomenogical tradition of sovereignty, the absolute, perception of the present in order to introduce an alternative or "natural" perspective that prepares the reader for Lingis's subsequent descriptions of people confronting their own circumstances. Like Agamben, Lingis is generally cautious about using the term "origin." He instead attempts to see how people conceive of their actions and deeds as bringing forth something new or, in Hacking's terms, moments of arising.

One example appears in "Innocence." Lingis mixes together variations of birth—from physical to spiritual. In this case the key term is "awakening." Our biological birth is already a freakish chance in nature. "The odds of being you are one in ten to the 2,400,000,000th power." As if addressing someone he knows, Lingis continues, "You were born and appear in the world as a will-o'-the wisp hovering above its interconnections and bearings." He adds:

What a stupendous marvel, your birth in a Reno hospital, in a dusty hut in a nameless favela! What a marvel, the newborn, the born new! And what innocence! How light is your birth, not laden with the weight of the past it has to answer for! In the past with all its crimes, all its outrages and villainy, there was nothing whatever of you.[18]

Then Lingis shifts to how awakening to the world is another kind of beginning. We awaken to new horizons or demands, unexpected lusts or commitments, fresh faces and difficult options. We become alert to what we previously took for granted.

Awakening is a break. Borrowing from Nietzsche about active forgetting, Lingis depicts awakening as an innocence that is active rather than passive. In his words, "Awakening is a commencement. It is a point of departure. We come alive, we become alive to the dragonfly, to the twisted grain of the porch railing. Awakening is a birth."[19]

Immature and Naïve Sciences

Hacking has referred to Foucault's work as immature science. This was not a derogatory aside about how the hard sciences are more empirical or rigorous in using methods of induction and deduction. Immature science in some ways is more challenging, for it tries to investigate the forms and developments of knowledge systems, particularly those that assert to present a study of human life. In the hard sciences the rules and criteria for determining what is true or false, which evidence is relevant or not, what counts as a persuasive demonstration are relatively stable in terms of analyzing the objects to be studied.

Not so with the sciences of human beings. There some of the very terms to be analyzed—madness, humane, reasonable, justifiable, labor, monstrous, normality, criminal—are subject to constant reevaluation. They and many other concepts about humans, according to Hacking, involve how "objects constitute themselves in discourse."[20]

Deathbound Subjectivity speculates on a science of the singular and a prophetic sense of future. This is not about a science of human nature. Rather, Lingis discusses actions and potentialities that have or still might exist. Some of these we might realize. But for those who might die for a cause, there can be no knowledge. As each death is singular, what could it mean to talk about a science of the singular? Lingis, commenting on Heidegger, answers by invoking heritage and the heroic. The heroic prepares and anticipates the heritage for someone else. Those who accomplish their "own potentialities delineate what is possible; the effectuation of their own mortal itineraries destines potentialities for others."[21]

Lingis extends this thought to many of his subsequent phenomenological descriptions. In recent interviews he surmises that there is an element of the naïve in his writings. At first the audience balks. How can an established college professor and author of many scholarly articles and books, not to mention a world traveler, claim to be naïve? The term "naïve" comes from the Latin word for "native." Although a derisive sense of naïve alludes to the ignorance of peasants and neophytes, there is a sense that naïve underscores those moments when we recognize or celebrate the native components of one another's lives.

When Lingis tells the stories of those in faraway lands or his home country, he goes native not in the ethnological sense of living with them. Rather, he reminds the reader that if he or she happened to be in Lingis's position, here's a thoughtful glimpse of what you also might be witnessing. His naïve writing is about describing and studying native moments in their passions, imperatives and visions.

Conclusion

This chapter has outlined several perspectives on genealogy as philosophy. "Why this, and not something else?" is a frequent question that drives genealogical inquiry. Why the ascetic rather than the hedonic ideal? Why the penitentiary rather than justice via mediation? Why an eighteenth-century discourse on preventing childhood masturbation rather than a pedagogy that encourages pleasures?

Since Nietzsche, genealogy has opened up a variety of explorations into the birth—and death—of human ideals.

It has examined shifts and breaks as well as the long lives of intellectual or moral continuities. But change or disruption does not just arise as part of the dynamics of competing discourses or power/knowledge frameworks and the exchange of experts and those who wield power. Human bodies are not merely creatures subjected to disciplines and ever emerging forms of biopolitics. Changes and transgressions are not only attributable to shifts in paradigms or intellectual disputes.

Change or transformation is also rooted in an existential moment by individuals who dared to say, "why this, and not something else?" Challenging how things are often springs from those who summon the courage, love, justice, boldness and even the willingness to die. Understanding these efforts cannot rely only on paradigms, networks and prevailing discourses. There are other value terms at stake. In Lingis's words, "Laughter and tears, blessing and cursing, give birth to the primary operative words—the value terms."[22]

Existential genealogy, as presented in much of Lingis's work, studies this birth. Hence his frequent accounts of humans who throw caution to the wind, dare the impossible, rise to action or leap into the unknown.

Notes

1. Friedrich Nietzsche, *On The Genealogy of Morals*, trans. Walter Kaufmann (New York: Vintage, 1989), I/17.
2. Giorgio Agamben, *The Signature of All Things*, trans. Luca D'Isanto with Kevin Attell (New York: Zone Books, 2009).
3. Friedrich Nietzsche, *Ecce Homo*, trans. Walter Kaufmann (New York: Vintage, 1989), 312-313.
4. Nietzsche, *Genealogy*, Preface, #2.
5. Ibid., Preface, #7.
6. Ibid,.
7. Ibid., I/17.

8.   Ian Hacking, "Michel Foucault's Immature Science", in his *Historical Ontology* (Cambridge: Harvard University Press, 2002), 97.

9.   Michel Foucault, *Discipline and Punish: The Birth of the Prison*, trans. Alan Sheridan. The ranking in philosophy cited the book's influence on political theory, social sciences and the possible ethical implications of the book's perspective on humanistic ideals. The ranking in criminal justice focused on the book's introduction to an entirely fresh perspective on studying crime, law enforcement and the development of experts and institutions responsible for explaining or controlling crimes. In this light, it seems unusual how an entire book on Nietzsche's *Genealogy* barely mentions Foucault, aside from Alisdair MacIntyre's essay that indicts Foucault's lack of normative standards in his critiques. See *Nietzsche, Genealogy, Morality*, ed. Richard Schacht (Berkeley: University of California Press, 1994).

10. Alphonso Lingis, *Sensation: Intelligibility in Sensibility* (Atlantic Highlands, NJ: Humanities Press, 1996). Foreword.

11. Nietzsche, *Genealogy...*, II/9.

12. Nietzsche, *The Gay Science*, #110.

13. Michel Foucault, *Wrong-Doing, Truth-Telling: The Function of Avowal in Justice*, trans. Stephen W. Sawyer (Chicago: University of Chicago Press, 2014), 217.

14. Foucault, *Discipline and Punish*.

15. Agamben, *The Signature of All Things*, 85.

16. Ibid., 87.

17. Lingis, *Deathbound Subjectivity*, Ch. 1.

18. Lingis, *Dangerous Emotions*, 104.

19. Ibid., 105-106.

20. Hacking, op. cit., 98.

21. Lingis, *Deathbound Subjectivity*, 124.

22. Lingis, *Dangerous Emotions*, 98.

Chapter Eight

Tomorrow Will Be Different

Truly, it is a blessing and not a blasphemy when I teach: 'Above all things stands the heaven of chance, the heaven of innocence, the heaven of accident, the heaven of wantonness.'

Lord Chance—he is the world's oldest nobility, which I have given back to all things; released them from servitude under purpose.

I set this freedom and celestial cheerfulness over all that like an azure bell when I taught that no 'eternal will' acts over them and through them.

Nietzsche, Before Sunrise[1]

You Will Be in Her Arms Again

"The Song of Innocence" introduces the reader to several individuals from Peru. The focus is on Nancy Gilvonio and Nestor Cerpa Cartolini. The author does not say how he knows them, as no sources or endnotes are provided. The central accounts of their lives span from 1988 to 1996. Lingis may have met them in his earlier travels or learned about them from Peruvian literature or film. He could also be organizing his thoughts from all the memories told and retold by the friends and acquaintances of these two individuals. At times without formal recognition he incorporates all three sources. Presumably, the vivid and detailed portraits of their lives suffice as confirmation.

Nancy Gilvonio's birth, childhood and early teen years appear as mishaps and singular moments. She helps feed and dress her younger brothers and sisters. Meanwhile, she starts to enjoy school and becomes relentless in all her studies. She sees how hard her father and brothers work on a small piece of land, recognizes that she will not follow her mother's shadows, and suddenly takes off to study at a regional university in hopes of becoming a teacher or professional. Her only belongings fit in a bag carried over her shoulder. When she returns home the likelihood of any semblance of continuity or promise seems abruptly threatened. It marks a break in her life, a break that "makes possible hope. Hope is hope by rejecting the evidence of the past, by being against all the odds."[2]

For upon her return home she discovers that the government soldiers without provocation invade citizens' houses, beat or torture her father and neighbors, cause friends and acquaintances to "disappear." She soon meets two brothers, Americo and Raul, who collaborate with her on insisting that this oppressiveness does not have to be. All agree that things could be better tomorrow and their fellow citizens can be released from servitude.

In this quest she meets Nestor Cerpa Cartolini, who has just escaped from prison and immediately tells her about his comrades whose eyes have been gouged or bodies burned. Immediately Lingis, as if writing to them, announces, "How fierce is your love!"[3] Here he clearly notes how hope is complemented by the drives of lust and beauty. "What is this great power," Lingis asks, "that makes us able to make love to this person this night as though we had never made love to anyone before to make love to this person this night as though there will never be anyone again?"[4]

On other nights they have to worry about being caught, helping fellow citizens or protecting their friends and families. In 1995 Nancy Gilvonio was arrested on charges of terrorism, convicted and placed in a harsh cell for life. No one heard from her thereafter. Soon her beloved Nestor Cerpa Cartolini is captured in quite different circumstances. He becomes part of a revolt to take over a prison and improve conditions for the inmates while addressing more fundamental social dangers and arbitrary arrests by the government that dares to impose its eternal will upon its own citizens. There is an initial bombing with numerous casualties, then relative peace and calm. The lovers no longer are sure about the whereabouts of each other, but by all accounts their love, like Heloise and Abelard, intensified during the separation. It remained part of their "passion for justice that flared in it is still seen."[5]

Four months after the violent prison take-over, negotiations over a hostage-for-prisoner exchange got bogged down. Many of the hostages, out of age, poor health or personal needs, were already released. The rest of them were treated well, often getting delicious meals from nearby restaurants and confident in their safety at the hands of the respectful rebels. So there was a minimal sense of urgency. This relative calm was shattered by a surprise attack when the military stormed the area and killed all the hostage-takers, including Nestor Cerpa Cartolini. The soldiers put an extra bullet through each of their heads to make sure.

A letter to his 9-year-old son was soon found. In it he does not bemoan his plight or offer a last-minute lecture on injustice. He instead writes to his son, "If I ever leave (here) it will be because I have achieved what you are waiting for and dreaming of: having your mummy out of prison, being able again to see her, touch her, play with her and be in her arms."[6]

Visions of What Hovers Before Us

Several exhibits and museums in England have featured the artistic works of two native brothers, Jake and Dino Chapman. Born in 1966 and 1962 respectively, they consider their endeavors to be a political collaboration, not in terms of taking sides on a particular political controversy, but in terms of inviting audiences to another way of seeing ourselves. The essay "Fake Fetishes, Disrobed Mannequins" elaborates on the directions of this collaboration.

Readers begin with a detailed description of a wooden sculpture carved by the Chapman brothers. From a distance it resembles an ancient African or Melanesian mask. On a closer look, one finds how the inner carvings actually resemble various icons of McDonald's — the golden arches, Ronald McDonald's red hair. The initial expectation of detecting fetishes among primitive art is displaced by the chance realization that the Chapmans are illuminating the fetishes of today, as found world-wide in fast food chains, conjuring the sights and smells of greasy burgers, stale burnt ashes and cheesy flavors.

A photograph of the Chapmans' "Zygotic acceleration, Biogenetic de-sublimated libidinal model" accompanies Lingis's experience and account of this work. They are 21 fiberglass resemblances of front-window girl mannequins one might find in any child's clothing store. Except here the mannequins are virtually nude, wearing only black tennis shoes. Their torsos and genitalia are blurred over, but some of the faces seem slightly contorted, bearing sexual parts rather than noses and mouths.

They invite the viewer to a deviant pleasure while highlighting a culture's taste for a marketing industry that recycles lustful figures of sculpted pre-pubescent girls selling the latest fashion. Imagine if these figures could be reproduced through the latest science. What might we see tomorrow? One possibility, Lingis draws from the Chapman's visions: "The libidinal model is of junk products of mass-fashion manufacture, merged into botched products of genetic engineering."[7]

From these and other works by the Chapmans, Lingis finds a range of thoughts and emotions. Much of it comes by chance.[8] Although the mix of filth and dysfunction, terror and pity, consumerist euphoria and pedophiliac desire conveyed in their works tempts one to an indictment of globalized cultures and the damning hypocrisies of political progress, Lingis finds that they provoke an unexpected laugh. For they get us to see what is so "blatantly in ourselves."[9]

This laughter is not ironic or derisive. It begins with the chance encounter of the Chapmans' work, and the laughter emerges from the viewer's knowledge gained in earlier chance encounters with the non-Western fetishes and we see how their work plays with and integrates aspects of a self. The laughter is centered on our persistent ideal of the rational and self-governing self, one that measures utilitarian goals and believes it is removed from the perverse pleasures depicted in some of the Chapmans' work.

In Lingis's words, alluding to a prehistory of the future, "The laughter that erupts and decomposes the moral autonomous individuality in us obscurely knows and calls forth a new kind of existence for us. Henceforth the question of what that existence will be hovers before us."[10]

Projects

These two stories are among many presented in Lingis's writing where people's visions and directions are geared toward another existence that awaits us. They show human beings immersed in a project. They attempt to change the present or envision a different future. Some fail, as both the young Nancy Gilvonio and Nestor Cerpa Cartolini were killed before ever seeing their child grow up or their fellow citizens more free. Some succeed, as with two brothers having their work displayed across England.

For Lingis, the notion of success or failure is relegated to secondary importance. First, the criteria to assess success or failure are often subject to endless disputes. For example (not from Lingis), the film "The Imitation Game", based on the life of Alan Turing, surveys a blend of inordinate success and abject failure. Philosophy teachers and artificial intelligence fans are quite familiar with Turing's enduring influence as one of the founders of the computer. "The Turing Machine" is a staple in courses and textbooks in challenging students to identify an essential difference between computer and human intelligence, and if unable then to conclude that the latter is neither unique nor inherently superior.[11] Though a cantankerous mathematical prodigy, Turing turned out to be a godsend to the British military in World War II. He was able to break the Enigma code, the system of complex secrets that Germans would communicate in order to plan attacks on Great Britain. Turing's perseverance and brilliance saved at least 15 million lives, 2 years of war and maybe even ensured the survival of an independent Great Britain.

In the early 1950s, Turing was suspected of being a sympathizer to the Stalin regime, but inadvertently the police came upon evidence that Turing was not a spy — far worse, he was guilty of "public indecent exposure," which in those days was a euphemism for being homosexual and considered a criminal deed. After the courts sentenced him to chemical castration instead of prison time, Alan Turing soon committed suicide. On what basis does one determine that such a remarkable life is considered a success or failure?

A second problem with assessing success or failure lies in the vague notion of where one exactly succeeded or failed. Whether one surveys historical developments in ideas, athletics, art or rock and roll, the notion of influence or legacy prevails. We debate or take sides on the great thinkers, who belongs in a sport's hall of fame, the relative rankings of the top books or most influential films of a century, which artists have been most enduring, or the rock stars whose work has spanned generations. Does this emphasis on success or avoidance of failure overshadow the intense realities — planned or unexpected — of all those who have committed to a project?

Lingis's response is in terms of honor and the ignoble. In a two-chapter section titled "Word of Honor", he surveys the multiple ways we utter or assert "I am a (fill in the blank)." These are not avenues following the dictum "Know Thyself." They are better seen as proclamations or affirmations of one's tasks, of those things he or she senses as important or urgent, of the possibilities that are emerging, or the chance for a departure.

Numerous examples are highlighted—from the dancer, shaman and doctor to Paul Gauguin and David Abram.

Regardless, is there not a risk that these affirmations are exercises in self-delusion, including being deluded by supporting a losing cause? Lingis acknowledges this risk, but counters that we nevertheless still recall or honor the "losers of history—Brutus and Montezuma, Gandhi and Che Guevara...If we continue to fight for a cause we know is lost, we do so to demonstrate to ourselves and our comrades and to those as yet unborn that the cause that is winning is ignoble."[12]

In part Lingis is responding to French philosopher Jean-Paul Sartre, who gave considerable attention to the idea of the project as part of human life. Sartre also cautioned against overemphasis on results, consequences, of the greatest good, but for reasons different from Lingis. For Sartre, the extent or level that a project stems from bad faith or a genuine act is more fundamental in terms of understanding our relation to time, space, others and oneself. As its etymology indicates, "pro-ject" is a going or throwing forward. Someone's project involves him or her, or they, anticipating a future that, says Sartre, reshapes their recognition of the present that will no longer be. This "not" is central to Sartre's view. It reflects not just the moment when one "intentionally realized a conscious project,"[13] but that this realization is anchored to the negative. To act initially has a sense of withdrawal from what is, an attempt to erase or negate it. Citing Spinoza's comment, "Omnis determination est negation," Sartre finds that one's existential actions or commitments are stirred by a negative sense—what is but should not be. Sartre writes, "There is a factual state—satisfying or not—only by means of the nihilating power of the for-itself."

The project is not initiated solely by being conscious of the negative, it is also an act of freedom. Arguing against both determinism (in which free will is an illusion and human actions are part of the cause/effect account that applies to everything else) and the substantive will (as the cause of subsequent deeds and actions), Sartre contends that freedom is the basis of this existential negative. His various examples, from the waiter and bricklayer to the holed-up rebel and fatigued comrade, distinguish moments of bad faith from instances of a meaningful project. Each embodies a struggle for freedom.

This struggle is not just a matter of someone or something curtailing our freedom; it also concerns one's effort in appropriation and to be complete or achieve totality. This is part of the absurdity of freedom. Each genuine act is kind of a beginning, but in Sartre's words, "A beginning which is given as the end of a prior project—such must be the instant. It will exist therefore only if we are a beginning and an end to ourselves within the unity of a single act...Now it is precisely this which is produced in the case of a radical modification of our fundamental project."[14]

Lingis advances Sartre's insights on the body, the singularity of a situation and the absurdity or hilarity that confounds so many human plights, but is skeptical of the existentialist emphasis on the negative, appropriation, the unity of the conscious self with its projects, and the absolute basis of freedom. The opening chapters of his first book already indicate his departures from central tenets of major existentialists. Lingis introduces a variety of forms of life—octopus, savages, coral reefs and their millions of inhabitants, Hindu lovers, body builders and deep-sea divers, among others.

Even a brief account of these forms shows how many actions are rooted in excess and an abundance of energy rather than a lack of force or negative sense of self. The notion that we appropriate that which we encounter is "derisible" in Lingis's terms, for it overlooks the likely fact that the encounter with an octopus, savage or deep-sea diver is not about my freedom or my project. Often we are just spectators and aliens to the object. "...I drift completely a stranger profaning a sphere of resplendent phenomena whose glory, utterly disinterested, call for no acolyte."[15]

While both Sartre and Lingis illuminate in detail cases of individuals committed to a cause, risking their well-being for a belief, acknowledging the possibility of disappointment that always lurks about, Lingis disagrees that unity or totality—whether anticipated or realized—is fundamental to the project. Sartre's phenomenological accounts mostly feature types of individuals who lack specific names for individuals at various levels of consciousness, bad faith and the centrality of freedom. Lingis highlights the faces and names of innumerable individuals in all sorts of surroundings and occasions.

This distinction is not just about a panorama of human beings as part of a philosophical story. In his attention to a detailed portrayal of the human beings, Lingis brings to light the importance of these lived encounters and how fragmented our lives can be—and maybe should be. Because these portrayals require their own descriptions and the truths and realities they introduce, Lingis hesitates to conclude that various factions of our lives have some central or unifying factor, such as freedom, community ideals or ego-centered motives. Here Lingis insists on the enduring significance of phenomenology. "Practical reality is open to a phenomenology that would describe the field of action as discovered by inhabiting it and by our movements, manipulations, and utilizations. The social field is open to a phenomenology that would describe the encounter with others as loci of appeals and demands and the associations formed with them."[16]

This approach to practical reality and the social field distinguishes Lingis not only from Sartre and other existentialist thinkers, but from other philosophical perspectives that would dismiss the practical reality or social field that comprises the projects of Nancy Gilvonio and Nestor Cerpa Cartolini, the Chapman brothers, among so many other associations. It is with these rather distant collaborations that Lingis presents fresh insights on what is true, good or beautiful.

Directives

Lingis says that to abide by this phenomenological approach involves "resisting all forms of holism. (It) holds that the directives we find in the night, the elements, the home, the alien spaces, the carpentry of things, the halos and reflections of things, the faces of fellow humans, and death have to be described separately."[17]

What are these directives? They are responses to the things and moments which grab one's eye and demand one's attention. A buddy takes the weekly load of dirty clothes to the laundromat and suddenly meets the love of his or her life while waiting for an available dryer. A major knee injury ends any chances of playing basketball in college, so the kid decides on chemistry and is now applying to grad school. You just learned that your family can be arbitrarily arrested or punished, and now you seek justice. I happen to wander into a used bookstore looking for a chess book or detective novel, and serendipitously discover the early works of a remarkable thinker. Friends and families start preparing 6 months in advance for next year's festival/spectacle, as the newest theme just got announced.

Directives are forces or perceptions that elude our control and pop up from a world that seems oblivious to our personal statue on this planet. Directives do change our lives, though in unpredictable and undefined ways, arising in some of the most mundane as well as extraordinary circumstances. They catch us off guard, help us forget our routines, absorb our attention morning till night, introduce something or someone more important than ourselves, celebrate another of life's wonders, or prepare to die for another.

For Lingis these responses often anticipate rather than follow the existentialist emphasis on freedom. The human movements stirred by these forces and perceptions often are not driven by intentions or purposeful actions. In his view, "... the movements of perception, both the controlled perception which is scientific observation, and the continual perception which is the scientist's, and our, life—are neither reactions and adjustments nor intentional and teleological acts, but responses. If perception is not a succession of mechanical determinisms, our perception exercises freedom because it obeys directives it finds in the environment."[18] Here we find that being free and obeying comprises a good part of what gives our lives meaning, substance and memorable thoughts.

Unlike most existentialist criticisms of determinism based on the centrality of freedom, Lingis shifts the criticism of determinism to the undetermined moments when a directive appears. No doubt we neglect or dismiss many that appear, never sure whether we can justify or revisit our choices. But on occasion we can't help but to respond. Or we choose to respond. Lingis tends to organize these directives under passions, visions and imperatives.

A passion is what moves us, a vision entices our future endeavors, and an imperative tells us what you or I must do at this particular moment. Lingis alters the language that depicts such moments. In his earlier writings he sees passions, visions and imperatives as aspects or attributes of a person. Later writings extend directives to natural settings and works of grandeur. For instance, reflecting on Te Pito O Te Hanua, or the Navel of the World, or what most Westerners call the statues of Easter Island, Lingis recounts "passions turned to fathomless distances that raised those stones into giant statues were drawn from the upsurge of the volcanoes themselves, that those vacant eyes reflected the radiance of the skies, that the song of the winds and the seas was on those lips, and that those great stone faces and their raiment held the color of the ardent lava and of the restless oceanic depths."[19]

Later writings focus more on impassioned energies and visionary bodies. Objecting to the view that the mind receives images, processes them in order to command the body's next movements, as well as the Freudian notion that our dreams harbor inner secrets or fears, Lingis depicts bodies that come alive when stirred by and stirring up visions. "It is not our minds detached from our sleeping bodies, but our eyes, lips, jaws, teeth, fists, thighs, penises, clitorises, and vaginas that are generating images, are dreaming."[20] They illuminate the excess and free energies of our bodies rather than the repressed memories of our tormented psyches.

The visionary body is discovered among infants, children, dancers, lovers, artists, walkers or comrades—in fact, among any of us. It is discovered still among the aged, as indicated by the photo of the old man from Irian Jaya, Indonesia, which introduces an essay on "Our Visionary Body." The visionary body is more than just corporeal and material. It extends to words and speech. What we imagine, dream of, read about or witness can also promise an element of the prophetic.

Following the essay on the visionary body, Lingis presents a short essay on "Oracular Words." Here words are more than components of rational communication, a way of categorizing ideas and beliefs, or utilitarian expressions about exchanging needs or wants. Words often have their own capability to heighten or intensify experiences. They consecrate what comes before us, whether by blessing some good fortune or cursing what is venal or malicious. In this sense Lingis writes, "Words too call up visions of things imminent or far-off. Brief words— 'dance,' 'mother,' 'on the road'—reverberate in the distances and a depth, striking up luminous apparitions and destinies."[21]

These words also comprise the stories we tell and retell about ourselves. Each time we modify or embellish the story, trying to make sense of what we decided to do or not do, understanding the coherence or interruptions that we have experienced. "As we project the plot of our lives into the coming days and years, we incorporate pure guesses, wishful thinking, and imaginative constructions."[22]

Again, though he infrequently uses the term project, Lingis's accounts invoke the etymology of the term. Namely, the visionary body and oracular words respond to directives that urge one forward. The visionary body and oracular words enable one to sense an imperative that only he or she can obey. This is one of the tasks of his existential genealogy. To describe human beings who anticipate and strive for a tomorrow where things might be different.

Notes

1. Friedrich Nietzsche, *Thus Spoke Zarathustra*, trans. R. J. Hollingdale (Baltimore MD: Penguin, 1961), Part III, #4, "Before Sunrise."

2. Lingis, *Trust*, 93.

3. Ibid., 97.

4. Ibid., 98.

5. Ibid., 98.

6. Ibid., 102.

7. Lingis, *Violence and Splendor*, 109.

8. Ibid., 106.

9. Ibid., 109.

10. Ibid., 109.

11. Andrew Hodges, *Turing* (New York: Routledge, 1999).

12. Lingis, *The First Person Singular*, 44.

13. Jean-Paul Sartre, *Being and Nothingness*, trans. Hazel E. Barnes (New York: Washington Square Press, 1966), 529, "Being and Doing: Freedom."

14. Ibid., 570. Though Lingis is most frequently associated with the work of Levinas and Merleau-Ponty in light of his translations, his relation to Sartre is also complicated. For a

closer look, see Lingis, "Freedom and Slavery in Sexuality", Ch. 1, in *Libido* (Bloomington, IN: 1985); "Intuition of Freedom, Intuition of Law", *The Journal of Philosophy* 79:10 (1982).

15. Lingis, *Excesses*, 9.
16. Lingis, *The Imperative*, 216.
17. Ibid., 3.
18. Ibid., 4.
19. Lingis, *Dangerous Emotions*, 23.
20. Lingis, *The First Person Singular*, 48.
21. Ibid., 50.
22. Ibid., 54. In a personal letter Lingis readily acknowledged, "I am full of projects..." See David Karnos, "Personal Correspondences", in *Itinerant Philosophy*, ed. George and Sparrow, 88.

Chapter Nine

Visions Reborn

In the end I must say: I see faces that belong to past generations; this region is studded with images of bold and autocratic human beings. They have lived and wished to live on: that is what they are telling me with their houses, built and adorned to last for centuries and not for a fleeting hour.
Nietzsche, Genoa.[1]

A Temple of Eros

Reflecting on the Kandarya Mahadeva Temple, Lingis introduces his essay "Khajuraho" with its picture. He opens with a lengthy passage from Henri Micheaux on erotic love and the Hindu practice of praying while naked, including his conclusion that for Hindus "...it would be worse to make love to a woman (in the European way) who individualizes you too much and does not know how to pass from the idea of love to that of Everything." The next ten pages of the essay have nothing to do with Micheaux or the temple.

Following this passage Lingis reviews several influential perspectives on erotic love. Covering classic views of Plato and Aristotle, as well as modern ideas from Freud, Lacan and Derrida, he concludes that the carnal passion has received an ambivalent or hostile reception. It tends to be regarded as either exclusionary (only this individual, and no other) or generalizing (everything can be subject to lustful urges, from sensual or natural symbols to weapons and military alliances).

He contends that efforts in explaining or understanding the carnal passion tend to obscure rather than clarify its varied realities. He considers how contrasting approaches, such as those of Plato or Freud, reach similar conclusions that "...the hypothesis that the search for knowledge, the striving for justice, the longing for beauty, the metaphysical nostalgia for unity and wholeness in the diversity and the transience of experience owe their force to genital rather than cerebral drives, represent transformations of or disguises of libido." [2]

Lingis examines four postulates or ideals about conventional takes on the erotic impulse. One is that there is an underlying or ultimate purpose (telos)—be it part of biological or social evolution—to sexual desires and acts. A second postulate or ideal holds that through erotic love we can come to a fuller understanding of who we truly are, thus keeping faithful to the "Know Thyself" ideal. A third postulate holds that the sex drive is creative as well as destructive. From infancy we learn to postpone or sublimate erotic passions until they can be properly channeled. A fourth theorizes that carnal passions ultimately seek an eternal ideal or metaphysical love, in which the erotic is abandoned or transformed into a metaphor.

Though at times skeptical, Lingis avoids a sustained counterargument against these familiar postulates and ideals. He does note that they are aligned in trying to minimize or erase the intense and erratic forces of erotic passions. Understandably a reader might tire of this disheartening review of familiar ideals and expect a substantive and positive rejoinder from Lingis. He can be somewhat evasive.

In *Libido*, though, his theoretical views take shape through an examination of the central ideas of influential Continental thinkers. In the last two chapters he particularly addresses how these thinkers nevertheless acquiesce to or indirectly agree with previous thought on the dangers and temptations of Eros. He relies on Levinas's ideas on alterity to highlight the shortcomings of recent French philosophers, including Sartre, Merleau-Ponty and Deleuze/Guattari. But they, including Levinas, present "no concept of the imperative, ordering sense of eros that is at work where an erotic sense is found embedded in geometrical reason, in architectonics, political economics, the destiny of a state, and the sense of the sacred..."[3] In this context Lingis asks: "Could one then imagine an eroticism that would spread everywhere, invade all domains of high culture, and not be a contagion of misery, not be driven by frustration?"[4]

Here the reader finally learns of Khajuraho. In this series of anonymous structures one visualizes eroticism as marvelous and pervasive. The existing monuments comprise a quarter of temples that still survive when built about 1000 years ago. Lingis notes the "intricate assemblages of porticos, cones, drums, towers, stalagmites, across which the mind is invited to follow the derivations of and correlations between a vast number of abstract forms..." The spectator will see "auto-erotic stimulation, dual and multiple cunnilinctio, penilincti, copulation, homosexual and bestial discourse circulate about the temple walls, without primacy of place or of artistry given to any figure."[5]

In this second part of the essay Lingis presents details about the materials and architectural designs and feats of the temples, theories of it being a microcosm of the universe or an integration of animal and human impulses. Those who have tried the math in calculating all the variables of the configurations and forms have estimated 8,400,000 possible sexual positions can be derived from the temple's facades. Body parts are depicted in unusual contexts and intermingling in surprising ways. Human, animal and divine members mix it up. Unlike the Socratic search for an eternal form in the erotic gaze, "Khajuraho shows the unending metamorphoses of forms before a gaze fixed in its own intensity."[6]

Contrary to the contagion of misery Lingis ascribes to our familiar views on carnal dangers, this temple devoted to eroticism spreads a contagion of passions and visions. These have circulated and been reborn for the millennium since some people decided to build this temple for those eyes the builders will never see. The visitor to this temple finds a beauty in the stones and configurations that has lasted for centuries, and the gods willing, another millennium or two. For tomorrow's or the next century's visitor will gain insight to another compelling presentation of love. In Lingis's more lyrical words, "But of course the carving is especially a vision. To be looked at, with eyes. With eyes of fish, of happiness."[7]

Recurrence in Existential Genealogy

So far the face-to-face encounter as presented through a variety of stories and reflections in Lingis's writings has drawn our primary focus. His here-and-now descriptions introduce the reader to unexpected circumstances and unpredictable consequences. This emphasis was meant to highlight how Lingis's accounts of human experiences anticipate what lies ahead, in contrast to Foucault's taking these experiences as routes to investigating their historical place in specific power/knowledge conditions.

There is considerable textual support for this emphasis. Lingis's translations of Levinas, perhaps the most influential philosopher on the face, set the tone for his own directions in describing human encounters that begin with the face-to-face moment. Many of his books contain at least one or two chapters with a title that includes "Faces", "Face to Face" or "The Face of (x)." Most of the photographs introducing various chapters briefly bring the eyes of the reader to the eyes of someone else, often from a distant part of the world. Even in photos where a natural landscape dominates, such as a glacier, desert or mountain, there usually appears, in relatively small scale, human figures going about their tasks.

This emphasis has inadvertently understated how the face-to-face moment seldom emerges from a vacuum or solely by happenstance. However dissimilar individuals might seem to one another when they first cross paths, what holds them together is a mutual recognition of a passion, vision or instinct that can be found in a remote past and somehow has caught the attention of the individuals. These might be conveyed through music, poetry, ritual, festival, sculpture, literature or the sacred. When individuals gain this recognition in one another, their lives embody a different self via a collaboration they were not expecting or a community of those who previously had nothing in common.

Lingis uses the terms recurrence or return to introduce such experiences.[8] He readily acknowledges the significance of Nietzsche here. The concept of eternal recurrence has been an enduring source of interpretation and dispute among Nietzsche's commentaries. Some consider it central to Nietzsche's metaphysics that in fact the cosmos does not have a destination but rather an endless repetition of the same. Others intertwine eternal recurrence with Nietzsche's views on the will-to-power, a view largely based on his posthumous works. A third perspective stresses an existentialist and hypothetical test for authenticity. That is, suppose you were to have this life again and again, would you still live it, or, if not, finally do something that made your life meaningful?

There is another option, according to Lingis. He sees in Nietzsche's sense of recurrence the historical fact that humans have always been reviving, reconceiving or redirecting their energies in relation to natural and divine forces. This fact is unfamiliar to those of us who consider the human condition as best represented in sedentary cultures—where we discuss history without embracing its moments of rebirth and dreams of a different tomorrow. We domesticated ones demarcate nature as wild or tamed.

The essay "Our Species: Premature, Symbiotic, Atavistic", illustrates how animal traits and human characteristics blend or intersect in numerous traditions and rituals throughout the world's cultures. Lingis employs Nietzsche's notion of the noble by stressing that this term refers to traits, forces or visions from the past that have, for whatever inexplicable reason, grabbed the attention of someone in some future time. Perhaps that someone is caught by the grandeur, courage, bravado, beauty that infiltrates the human-animal symbiosis. Or someone is moved by a divine vision or sacred place, becoming fascinated with what Nietzsche claims to be the noblest of traits — truthfulness.

Lingis underscores the point that Nietzsche's sense of the noble is not about ranking classes or privileges that anchor so many human associations (and scholarly disputations on Nietzsche). He contends that Nietzsche sees the rebirth or resurgence of ancient instincts and visions in his own observations of nineteenth century Europe. While Nietzsche often uses these cases as a way of undermining or questioning the ideals of his own time, Lingis does not conclude that this confirms the familiar view of Nietzsche as "systematic cynicism." He insists there is a more affirmative lesson to draw, "Nietzsche argues that the return of ancient instincts and pleasures produces new excellences."[9]

Extinct and Reborn

The rebirth of such productions does not necessarily bode well for social progress or political harmony. Frequently the recurrence of visions and instincts that initiate these rebirths are excessive, rebellious, outcast or anomalous. When Lingis characterizes such notions as premature or atavistic, he highlights how some truths or ideals are outside their own time. They hark from the distant past or dream of some lofty tomorrow while never seeming to be at home in the present.

Deferring to religious motifs, Lingis points out how many gods have died and been reborn. Nietzsche's declaration that "God is dead...and we are his murderers" is less a confession of atheism or nihilism than a critique of those who have corrupted some of the most ancient religious passions and visions by hateful revivals, malicious popes and malevolent proselytizers. If so, then to what extent do we affirm or denounce the array of instincts or visions offered by religion?

One possible answer from Lingis begins with his coming across human femur bones that have been well preserved. They seem to have been central to some shamanist ritual or preserved from the sacrifice of young virgins, according to historiographers and anthropologists. They are difficult to obtain and pass through customs. Etchings and carvings of the bones indicate they were meant to be played as horns for a sacred ceremony. They are now preserved in a museum or sold to tourists who will take them home to display for friends and visitors. Holding them may evoke images of monks and holy processions. Yet, admits Lingis, we can only wonder and be marveled by visualizing the intense sounds the bones made when played at a funeral or festive ritual. To hear those sounds in this context must have penetrated the souls of numerous ears while stirring their thoughts of the gods or divine truths. Perhaps, surmises Lingis, the sounds could also penetrate those souls who are not guided by such gods.

In this light Lingis proposes that the instincts or visions of these religious forces could be eventually detached from the central targets of religious belief while maintaining or invigorating its surprises and intensities. "In this way," he writes, "they can mask even from themselves their religious character. They can take hold of the sphere of art, of politics, or even the sciences, driving them with religious fervor and furor."[10] Here he cites Nietzsche in *Human, All Too Human,* who proposes art could be the domain if it "takes over a host of moods and feelings engendered by religion...communicating exultation and enthusiasm as it formerly could not."[11] As if carrying on a dialog with Nietzsche, the chapter "The Return of Extinct Religions" closes with the possibility of shifting attention from the god instinct to that of the nature, history, ancient bones and stones.

One instance of this fervor appears in ecstatic moments, such as when a traveler becomes overwhelmed by Petra. Nestled among mountains, gorges and barren lands in what is now called Jordan, Petra is a series of temples carved onto steep cliffs. Except for a small room or two, there is no place to reside. It is simply a façade. Two thousand years old, it was likely built by a nomadic group called the Nabateans. It remains uncertain whether the magnificent etchings were meant to be royal tributes, mausoleums or halls for rituals and ceremonies. Lingis recounts its history, how different tribes or nations took over the area, often destroying parts of the temple. There have also been earthquakes, floods and harsh weather that take a toll on the rocks and stones that make up the figures, columns and arrangements.

Visitors to the temples of Petra often realize an ecstasy of vision. To see the mix of figures presenting wild animals, humans and divine creatures stirs thoughts and imaginations. It also induces a typical ecstatic effect—loss or forgetfulness of self. "Before this epiphany you lose sight of yourself, you are this ecstasy of vision."[12] A visitor to these facades could learn from pamphlets about all the different occupants of the area, whether to celebrate or destroy the temples. A scholar might study the various interpretations of the structure or reasons for its construction in light of the most recent methods or theories about sacred works of art.

Lingis finds this helpful but incomplete. To look at the magnificence and perfection of this work built by these nomads, he adds, one senses that a vision or passion that was extinct is in fact reborn. It is reborn when someone 2000 years after its creation encounters…"facades behind which there are no rooms or passageways, only the immense darkness of inert rock, and our vision is held on a surface behind which there is the unthinkable."[13]

The Splendor of Birth

Existential genealogy, as with other Nietzsche-based genealogies, addresses the emergence or birth of a phenomenon that fascinates but eludes conventional analysis. Foucault looked at conditions of power and knowledge to situate such a birth, hence his titles on the birth of the clinic, human sciences or the prison. Lingis presents a different perspective. He studies the beginnings of a phenomenon in order to uncover unexpected directions. His study interweaves two parts. He first looks carefully at the face-to-face encounter as a moment that anticipates a canvass of possibilities. And second he finds how so much of this canvass comes by chance, good or bad fortune, while they derive their impetus from the revival of passions and visions of recent ancestors and ancient times.

In numerous chapters of *Violence and Splendor*, terms such as death, war, violence and filth appear in the titles. Most of what Lingis describes has very little to do with actual war or violence. Unlike readers who likely live in a country where bloody and cruel warfare is a regular component of their daily news, those depicted in these chapters shed very little blood. Most of his examples are about groups of people who have rituals for dancing and playing music that signal a readiness for war, engaging in dramatizations with colorful garb that enact a potential battle with a neighboring adversary, but in the end very little actual warfare. And certainly nothing close to the prevalence of violence and war of more civil and progressive nations.

Lingis introduces the Mount Hagen Show in Papua New Guinea as a case study. He situates it in a tumultuous history, its modest origins eventually giving way to a tourist and commercial bonanza for the government. In earlier times they did signify preparations for battle with rivaling tribes, regardless of how little blood was actually shed. He observes the participants singing, chanting and dancing in celebration. They are "splendid with the nacreous shells of mollusks, the skeletons and fangs of serpents, the tusks of boars, the teeth of flying foxes, the plumes of birds." [14] Through such moments there is not an issue of calculations of long-term self-interest or production of social harmony. "It is not the individual that willfully constructs these feelings in himself; the ancient passions themselves return."[15] These returns are greeted and experienced as births.

In an earlier account that related Nietzsche's eternal recurrence to the will-to-power, Lingis insists that it is not a theory but "an experience of high intensity." It is an experience that interweaves remembering and forgetting. It is Dioynsian in terms of its exuberance and selective in terms of what it wills to affirm. Citing Nietzsche's published and posthumous writings, he asks how many ideals and gods are still possible. Years before *Excesses*, he links the religious instinct with the god-formed instinct.[16]

Lingis also addresses how this religious instinct might not need to concern itself with new gods. He frequently extends the intensities and senses of the sacred to nature and non-human creatures. His comments on the Mount Hagen Show illuminate this shift. There is less focus on the divine and more on the natural elements that find splendor in a new birth of animal-like colors, powers, passions and impulses. "More profoundly...the instincts and emotions of our animality return. Behind instincts and emotions that are generated by culture Nietzsche found the wolf, cave bear, camel in us..."[17]

This return of an instinct or vision is not so simple, regardless of whether its latest version stems from new gods and ideals or still surprising kinships with natural elements and non-human creatures.

The birth of the Mount Hagen Show has a prehistory. Though it officially began in 1964, the political, cultural and military efforts leading to this year are full of intrigue, duplicity, tradition as well as unexpected greed, nationalism and economics. Following a concise review, Lingis describes the circumstances and local perspectives of the life of the Mount Hagen Show. Disputes abound. Years before it was celebratory and authentic, but now it is too touristic or still represents a tradition, or the government sees it as a cash cow or a public symbol of ancient respect, or it is nostalgia for old people or ignored by younger generations.

Clearly more money was involved. Ticket prices soared over 300 percent and endorsements from international brands became ubiquitous. Our cynical side might dismiss the show in its current state as a joke. Once again commercialism overtakes the sacred in the on-going battle of ideals and strengths.

Lingis counters this cynical twist by describing the dances, costumes, drum beats, festive reenactments that are conveyed by so many different people and, contrary to rumors, by people of all ages. As before, many of their displays continue to depict humans embracing animal or natural forces. "The men and women marching, dancing, filling the air with cries and chants under Mount Hagen, are splendid with the nacreous shells of mollusks, the skeletons and fangs of serpents, the tusks of boars, the teeth of flying foxes, the plumes of bird. It is not humans who invented splendor."[18]

Affirmations

The existential genealogy of Lingis extends from reborn visions of gods and ideals to the recurrence of animal passions and splendors in human celebrations and rituals. He acknowledges that many of these visions and passions arise when social representations or conventions no longer welcome them. They tend to be thoughts out of season. Thus there remains a skeptical challenge that genealogy is little more than celebration of the eccentric and unusual with no pertinent contribution to current social and political controversies and dilemmas[19]. This criticism has certainly been attributed to Foucault's take on genealogy, particularly when his position made public his respect for the ascension of the Ayatollah Khomeni as a spiritual and political revolutionary. This challenge treats Foucault as a clever gadfly, but hardly a beacon for optimistic political directions.

In Lingis's case, this criticism poses different risks because, unlike Foucault who focuses on unusual episodes and events within European history, many of Lingis's stories and characters appear in times and locales far remote from European history. Are these cases little more than endearing but anomalous anecdotes and case studies that are cherry picked to mock or undermine the ideals and practices that also draw Foucault's attention? A skeptic's answer could easily say that Lingis's case, regardless of the relation to Foucault, bears tantalizing similarities to the fanciful counterexamples presented by analytic thinkers to undermine a major theme or argument. Granted, analytic counterexamples may be more far-fetched and Lingis's more realistic, but that hardly seems a significant contrast.

These critiques conflate the genealogies of Foucault and Lingis when in this context they digress. This is apparent in their respective departures from Nietzsche. For Foucault the *Genealogy of Morals* is the anchor to his studies of institutions and power/ knowledge networks that arise with noble intentions, only to find their proliferation through the enhancements of disciplines, bio-powers, therapeutic authorities, among others. Nietzsche saw his three genealogical inquiries as exposing the cruelty, guilt and shame that were used as psychological tools for a way of living and thinking. For they showed a rather shameful fact— that humans "would rather will nothingness than not will."[20] When pressed through interviews on current political struggles, Foucault was always reluctant to spell out or articulate plans or models of response for those who were willing to risk their bodies and lives in any political resistance.

The anchor to Lingis's existential genealogy is Nietzsche's *The Gay Science*. Looking at the Mount Hagen Show from a skeptical angle, one sees another loss of ethnic purity to global capitalism. Lingis sees a moment of excess and exuberance. There are in these shows and so many other rituals, ceremonies, temples and performances glimpses of a future humaneness. Section #337 of *The Gay Science* is cited in order to introduce joyful excesses rather than disciplinary powers of the Mount Hagen Show.

This affirmation of existential genealogy is found through many of the individuals, stories and traditions animating Lingis's philosophical explorations. He is not very specific on how they offer rational proposals on current controversies and problems. But he is quite specific in illuminating the possibilities that still await us humans. As some of the quotes above indicate, Lingis's existential genealogy anticipates, among others, the eyes of fish and of happiness, visions that transport us to the unthinkable, and ancient passions that produce new excellences.

Notes

1. Nietzsche, *The Gay Science,*291.
2. Lingis, *Excesses*, 50-51.
3. Lingis, *Libido*, 118-119.
4. Lingis, *Excesses*, 58.
5. Ibid., 59.
6. Ibid., 66.
7. Ibid., 67.
8. Lingis, see *Body Transformations*, Ch. 2, and *Trust*, 149-161.
9. Lingis, *Body Transformations*, 150.
10. Lingis, *Trust*, 158.
11. Ibid., 205. Also see Nietzsche, *Human, All Too Human.*
12. Lingis, *Trust,* 23.
13. Ibid., 28.
14. Lingis, *Violence and Splendor*, 141.
15. Ibid., 146.
16. Alphonso Lingis, "The Will to Power", in *The New Nietzsche,* ed. David Allison (New York: Delta Books, 1977), 60-61.
17. Lingis, *Violence and Splendor*, 147.
18. Ibid., 147.

19. See Janet Afary and Kevin Anderson, *Foucault and the Iranian Revolution: Gender and the Seduction to Islamism* (Chicago: University of Chicago Press, 2005). The authors study Foucault's popular essays celebrating the emergence of a spiritual revolution in 1979 Iran led by the Ayatollah Khomeni. From two brief visits and scholarly research, Foucault endorsed the end of the Shah of Iran's reign of terror upon his own people. Afary and Anderson criticize Foucault for neglecting how this revolution was a throwback to earlier times when Islamic cultures treated women harshly and as second-class citizens. This is not merely a mistake of Foucault's rush to judgment. Rather, this is symptomatic of his historical genealogy as a politically inept philosophy.

20. Nietzsche, *On The Genealogy of Morals*, III, 28.

Excursus

Criteria for determining the significance of an artist, musician, scientist, thinker is an invariable hot topic for fans as well as specialists. One recurring criterion emphasizes the extent that the individual(s) in question has helped us to pursue our own investigations into new fields of experience or scholarship.

Daniel Dennett encourages readers and students to treat his and other philosophers' writings as open-ended introductions and conceptual toolboxes for our own distinct inquiries. If we find several ideas helpful or insightful, Dennett recommends that using them as "a springboard into your own exploration of the questions and answers that have been worked on for so long by so many thinkers."

The work of Foucault has spawned a variety of research directions. For example, Ian Hacking's studies on the taming of chance, mad travelers, social and natural kinds have helped me understand Foucault's ideas more clearly and how they can function as intellectual toolboxes. After completing scholarly pieces on Lingis as well as the *Encounters* project, I was curious if his writings could act as signposts for my own inquiries. If so, then maybe other readers of Lingis also could deploy some of his insights into their own experiences of fields of research.

The following two chapters attempt to use existential genealogy as a departure point for two separate studies. Each focuses on a prehistory, what Agamben says is probably the most exciting aspect of a historical event. Each study incorporates other central components of Lingis's perspective: chance encounters, unexpected twists, passions, vision, project, expenditure and moments of intensity in which one's self was suspended, transformed or briefly forgotten. The subjects in these attempts are members of my pantheon of human beings who have brought joy or insight to some of our lives.

The one on the birth of a band was more conscious. There are many books on The Beatles, but only recently there have been extensive biographies of their pre-fame days. The authors went to Liverpool's archives and interviewed those in Liverpool who witnessed the early days and the intense excitement and fun as the band began mastering a new kind of music. I published several op-ed essays on The Beatles in my local newspaper, but as famous and enduring artists. With Lingis's ideas as guidelines, this chapter explores the surprising twists and turns that led to 1964.

Earl "The Pearl" Monroe was my boyhood basketball idol. He played 4 years in my hometown, Baltimore. I saw most of the home games he played, and hopelessly tried to imitate his moves on the basketball court. He was once asked if he could teach some college players his moves, and Monroe replied, "No, because I don't even know how I make them!" He was traded to New York where he played the rest of his career. Monroe is in the basketball hall of fame and selected as one of the top 50 NBA players ever.

My research on his college years in part started out of curiosity, and in part because I simply wanted to try a "Lingis-like" project. At the time, I was not thinking about terms such as prehistory or chance events, which I already did with my Beatles inquiry. Here I conducted interviews, though several people were understandably quite guarded about talking to a stranger about their long-time friend. When they knew I was not a tabloid journalist looking for dirt on a famous person, they warmed up and offered some anecdotes about Monroe when he was a teenager and college student. I went to Winston-Salem to study rare television footage and newspapers from the late 1960s.

I was quite fortunate to have an interview with Mary Garber. She was in a nursing home and reluctant to have visitors other than family. But her eyes brightened up and her face cheered when she had a chance to talk about Monroe's college years at Winston-Salem State Teachers College. She was white, and probably the first female sports journalist to cover a men's athletics event. She reminisced about Coach Gaines, the social-political climate of the 1960s, the wonderful humans who graduated from the college. When my essay was published in one of the premier college basketball venues of the country, I sensed that Lingis's ideas could spawn further kinds of research.

Hence the following two chapters are central to my attempt to grasp his work.

Chapter Ten

Lennon/McCartney and the Birth of a Band

Once we determine to trust someone, there flows a current of strength and lightness and a distinctive freedom. We celebrate our trust in one another in our adventures, feasting, games of glamour, courage, skill, and in epic, song, poetry, and thought.
Lingis[1]

Chance Encounter at a Church Lot

They first met on a chilly Sunday afternoon at a church parking lot in 1957. The older one, John Lennon, had just finished a musical gig with his band, The Quarrymen. A mutual buddy introduced him to Paul McCartney, who at 15 years old seemed like a kid to the 17-year-old Lennon. They chatted about music and departed with some vague notion of getting together.

They were initially a bit wary of one another. Paul had just seen The Quarrymen perform and was impressed with John's singing and daring in a scarcely attended performance on this chilly Sunday afternoon on a parking lot. And John knew songs that Paul thought only he knew among all the teenagers in Liverpool. John was a bit jealous that Paul could read musical notation and tune a guitar. He was also surprised by Paul's knowledge of music, as it extended from what was currently popular to the sounds of their ancestors.

They soon met again and talked more about music, bringing their guitars and playing snippets from their favorite songs. At the ages of 17 and 15, John and Paul were veritable juke boxes insofar as the ranges of songs they could play. One might mention a Hank Williams tune, and the other would play some chords from the piece. Paul's parents always played music, his father performing in numerous Liverpool locales. John's mother,

Julia, who did not raise John, was a devoted fan of all kinds of music and encouraged John by giving him a guitar and teaching him some of her favorites. Paul's father was glad to see Paul develop an affinity for music as long as he kept his focus on a managing or teaching career. John's Aunt Mimi, who raised him, offered advice to John that was not prescient: "The guitar's all right for a hobby but it won't earn you any money." [2] These adult admonitions went unheeded.

A Prehistory to an Event in Song, Poetry and Thought

Within weeks something changed. John and Paul met again and realized a common passion—American music. Paul could sing Little Richard while John had Elvis down pat. They even played together the first rock and roll song to reach number one on the Billboard charts, Bill Haley and the Comets' "Rock Around the Clock." As the friendship quickly blossomed, they soaked up every piece of music available, be it on radio, 45s at the nearby record store, or local performances. Invariably their focus stayed on American artists. They heard, memorized and learned to perform the music of Chuck Berry, Buddy Holly, Smokey Robinson, girl groups, Carole King, Ray Charles, among many others. These American artists were gods to John and Paul. They were expending their brilliance and talent to two young men on another continent.

John and Paul became inseparable. "Soul mates" or "brothers" are how Liverpool's denizens recall them. They played as many gigs as offered, cut school to practice, visited local pubs and stores to hear the latest musical developments. Should they hear of a new single from the States they really appreciated, such as The Shirelles' "Baby, It's You" or Barrett Strong's "Money", John and Paul would immediately buy the music sheets and learn the lyrics and notes so they could perform it at their next gig. They even took some stabs at writing their own songs, simple ditties about who loves whom and whose hearts get broken.

Soon they decided on a lead guitarist, a shy, young and talented George Harrison, who shredded his fingertips because he practiced so much. John's close friend, Stuart Sutcliffe, became another guitarist. Another chum named Pete Best joined the group as the drummer. A small legion of loyal teenage fans developed, always excited in anticipating the group's next lunch time performances in the cellar of the Cavern Club or evening gigs in the basement setting of the Casbah Coffee Club. They kept tinkering with the group's name.

In 1960 Lennon and McCartney with their fellow band mates took off to perform at Hamburg, Germany. It was a 2-month stint in a foreign land they knew nothing about. Their parents were horrified. Paul, with his knowledge of music and the arts, could become a teacher. George was only 17 with a talent for a trade, but now clearly corrupted by the older John and Paul. And John, if he could stay out of jail, had potential to be an artist or writer. This is not possible, the parents would bemoan to themselves; that our boys are squandering away their future.

Hamburg was an eye-opener. The band dressed like reckless thugs as if aliens from a remote planet. They were loud, boisterous, outrageous—the German crowds loved them. John and Paul and their band played 6 days a week, from early evening to whenever the pubs closed in the next morning's wee hours. Their living quarters were little better than a prison, with two bunk beds, a chilly room and the bathroom and shower down the hallway. Drunks, pimps, whores, ex-Nazis, derelicts, mobsters, addicts were among the misfits attending their performances. Sailors from the nearby port or local adults strolling through the red light district would often stop by and see what the music was about. Fights broke out, spectators applauded or ridiculed the band's antics, pills were easily circulated, particularly uppers or speed (Benzedrin or Preludin) for the performers so that they could continue playing. John and Paul and the band drank on stage, getting as drunk as the spectators.

Amid this bedlam a young photographer, Astrid Kirschner, became captivated by their music. She befriended them and taught them different ways to pose before a camera, even introducing them to the "Exis", an abbreviated reference to existentialists in terms of youthful attitude, cool defiance and intense commitment rather than formal philosophy. She tried various looks with their hair, showed them how to use their eyes and face when looking into the lens, as if they were looking directly at their audience. And she and Stu immediately fell in love.

Regardless, Stu wrote to his Liverpool friend near the end of the Hamburg experience echoing what the band went through. "I came for a reason I do not know. I have no money, no resources, no hopes, I'm not the happiest man alive. Six months ago I thought I was an artist. I no longer think about it...Last Monday night, my night off, I wandered along the streets here, going mad with the beauty, just wandering and wandering by the docks... Beggars sleeping in doorways unconsciously scratch their lice-infested bodies. Drunken prostitutes lying on newspapers in the gutters slippery with garbage and ships excrement..."[3]

Despite such stretches of despair, the band also relished opportunities and surprises. Many nights John hurled back insults to the audiences, mocking the Nazi misfits and raucous drunks. Then Paul calmed the rambunctious crowds by schmoozing them with a tender ballad or two, such as "Over The Rainbow" or "Till There Was You." A nightclub manager often shouted for them to "Mach Schau!", German for keep playing and put on a show. John would make faces and wear a toilet seat around his neck, while Paul would start blaring lyrics of Little Richard or Jerry Lee Lewis. If they sensed the audience was approaching delirium, they'd engage a 15-20 minute rendition of Ray Charles' "What I'd Say." For their one day a week break, they partied in Hamburg's infamous Reeperbahn or attended other venues to see what kind of music was going on.

Throughout they played, practiced, wrote and played some more. Should any members of the band worry about money, girlfriend back home, parents' disapproval or missing school, Lennon would castigate them with his words. "Forget that... You're in a fuckin' band now!"[4] John and Paul realized that individual selves were lost among this new project. They realized they were now committed to what eventually and unexpectedly became a musical event: The Beatles.

A Current of Strength, Lightness and Freedom

When The Beatles returned to Liverpool, they were exhausted, emaciated, appearing to their families and friends as if they had been in a tragedy or war where food and cleanliness were unattainable. For 2 months they had been living in prison-like living quarters in Hamburg, with two bunk beds in a small room, always chilly and damp, with lingering stenches of cigarette smoke and dirty laundry. John and Paul wondered if it was over. They questioned their abilities, energies and willingness to continue. Maybe the adults were right after all—this rock 'n roll stuff is only a hobby. After several weeks off John and Paul got in touch with the rest of The Beatles and started rehearsing. They still had some bookings and always kept their word. They regrouped and returned to their favorite Liverpool venues, not sure if they had anything new to offer.

Their fans welcomed them back—only to be awestruck. This was not the same group. Before Hamburg, The Beatles were entertaining and fun. They were now otherworldly.

Fans heard and felt a sound never experienced before. It was loud, harmonious, precise, joyous. To hear them you felt glad to be alive. Bob Wooler, a booking agent who contracted The Beatles for a variety of venues, recalls one of their first performances after returning from Hamburg. The hundreds of fans packing the place "were transfixed...They hadn't seen or heard anything like it before. I'd never seen anything like it. The Beatles were sensational...They had such a magical influence on people. They put everything into their performance...They (The Beatles) were all stomping like hell and the audience went **mad**."[5]

It was an explosion. The Liverpool fans who remembered the pre-Hamburg Beatles witnessed a complete transformation. From numerous interviews with eyewitnesses, Bob Spitz likens it to a Messerschmitt hitting an unsuspecting target. The pounding of The Beatles sound took the form of rhythmic waves, a veritable assault on the audience. "There was nowhere to take cover on the open floor. All heads snapped forward and stared wild-eyed at the deafening ambush. The music crashing around them was discernibly a species of rock-n roll but played unlike they had ever heard it before. *Oh ba-by, yeahhhh/now ba-bay, wooooooo...* It was convulsive, ugly, frightening, and visceral in the way it touched the crowd."[6]

Word soon spread and fans began exchanging familiar questions: Where are The Beatles appearing next? Which lunch time coffee venue, which late evening club? Who's your favorite? Ignoring fire hazard warnings among overcrowded places, fans were squeezing into any open space to catch a Beatles performance. Many were swaying with their dates, while others danced and jumped about. Those fans closest to the stage simply stared and listened. Young workers would take an extra hour or two off from the job to enjoy both noontime performances. Weekend fans started arriving an hour or two early to secure the best spot to watch them. At times lines starting forming for venues not prepared for such ambitious audiences. And every 10 or 15 minutes, those waiting to get in the club would whisper to one another more familiar questions: Did you see them? Are The Beatles going to be on time? How are they looking?

This is 1960-61, years before the official Beatlemania of 1964 when they were nicknamed the Fab Four and appeared on the *Ed Sullivan Show* to the largest television audience ever. The eventual birth of The Beatles event had its beginnings in a more primordial orgy of sensations, as those immersed in these early performances felt, heard, smelled, danced to and were momentarily entranced by an unexpected reality. Given the remarkable repertoire and imagination of John and Paul in their early twenties, fans might be reminded of Heraclitus's insightful quip about never stepping into the same river twice, since fans never saw the same Beatles performance twice.

Consider one gig at the Cavern Club. With rudimentary wiring and old circuits, often a fuse would blow and the sound system and main lights went dead. In the dank basements of the Cavern Club, this would usually mean the end of the performance and panicky flight by the crowds. Not with The Beatles. As emergency lights still cast some dim and indirect light, they stayed on the stage and continued to entertain. John and Paul would improvise with antics, brief musical solos, singing snippets from favorite childhood songs the audience grew up with, then get their fans—none of them left— engulfed in the cellar shadows to join in and sing key words of the next song. Not panic, but another fascinating twist with the band. When the fuses were finally replaced so the lights and amplifiers came on again, The Beatles and their fans immediately returned to rock music and more pandemonium.[7]

Part of the joy for fans was that The Beatles were their secret. While the rest of the world fretted about a cold war, foreign battles to save colonialism, tiresome television game shows and fears of the collapse of democracy, teenagers in Liverpool knew they were the only ones with an experience that made life on this planet a bit sweeter, if not life-altering.

Upon a second trip to Hamburg The Beatles realized some decent money could be made as performers. When they returned again to Liverpool agents and scouts began hustling for larger audiences and more bookings. Then Brian Epstein stepped into the basement of the Cavern Club, became enthralled, and offered to be their manager. He was a local businessman who owned a record store and who was quite familiar with different ways to promote a product or talent.

Brian decided to promote The Beatles across the country in several ways. He extended the geographic horizons of their performances, sometimes a day's ride from Liverpool. He used his marketing skills to publish news blurbs in regional magazines about this unknown but exciting band from the north of England. Posters announcing every forthcoming Beatles concert appeared in Brian's store. He even went to the cultural center of England, London, and promoted The Beatles to several entertainment executives, though Brian knew their reputation to sniff at and turn their eyes away from anything produced in a forlorn city like Liverpool. Soon Brian persuaded the band to drop the black leather wardrobe and wear suits with matching coats and ties, as this would appeal to a wider audience. Most of all, Brian Epstein, after numerous rejections, secured The Beatles a recording audition with a major record label.

To the dismay of a coterie of devoted fans in Liverpool, the secret was out. And the rest, as they say, is history.

Celebrating Trust

The act of trust is a leap into the unknown.
Lingis[8]

Joshua Shenk presents John Lennon and Paul McCartney to be historical figures—as collaborators, not individuals. According to Shenk, the primary unit begins with a pairing in which each half magically brings out the creative and imaginative forces of the other. Shenk uses the electricity metaphor to account for the dynamic of these pairings, and draws his insights from a variety of examples: scientists Marie and Pierre Curie, philosophers Jean-Paul Sartre and Simone de Beauvoir, magicians Penn & Teller, DNA researchers Crick and Watson, among many others.

The pairing becomes more of a confluence insofar as the individual identities or private selves begin to merge. But they are not mirror images of one another. Each contributes distinct insights and talents to the pairing. Their collaborations become projects, yet these projects are entirely unpredictable. According to Shenk, however fragile, disruptive and wild a pairing can become, invariably, he concludes, there is an essential trait that involves a complete and intense trust in one another. Speaking about Lennon/McCartney, Shenk writes, "Whatever the pair's age or experience, this is a common quality at the outset, because the dawn of a connection presents a daunting mix of potential and uncertainty. Confluence means giving something up, leaping into an unknown."[9]

When John and Paul realized that they might go from performers to recording artists, they were leaping into the unknown, just as they did in their first venture to Hamburg. Brian told them to write some new songs, rehearse their best covers, and show up at the recording studio on time. In the words of Mark Lewisohn, in May 1962 things suddenly changed. "This was the moment when John Winston Lennon (21 years, 7 months) and James Paul McCartney (19 years, 11 months) looked each other full in the face and saw that *something*, saw white-hot ambition, determination, daring, craving, personality, talent and ego, and went for it."[10] At such a young age John and Paul were already being recognized in northern England as having a certain mastery of a new kind of music. Within 2 years this mastery would be embraced across the world.

In *Foreign Bodies* Lingis considers strange lusts and alien feelings that are our own. Describing a range of rituals, pedagogies of pleasures, practices of corporeal affirmations, Lingis cites Foucault's *The History of Sexuality* in order to open up alternative cultures of an "ars erotica." This was not just about the pleasures of lust. Rather, "ars erotica" provided a framework to attempt to interpret aspects of our lives that were works of art. Foucault's framework reaches back to ancient Greek and Romans as well as the Christian Fathers. Lingis's framework extends to more recent and remote regions of the planet.[11] What distinguished Lingis's focus is that in investigating the strange lust and alien feelings in remote times and places we unexpectedly discover passions and directions in ourselves that seem to have been forgotten or displaced.

When The Beatles arrived in America, they adeptly conveyed to their new-found audiences the music that was alien and strange to them—but their own! The Beatles themselves knew little about the United States other than what they saw on TV and movies. They may have had a vague idea of segregation and how disc jockeys such as Alan Freed or producers like Phil Spector overtly integrated music from different races. They did not know that there were record charts for contemporary and race music, that radio stations played only white music or gospel/blues music, or that public facilities had signs for "colored only."

So when their music was initially heard by American audiences, The Beatles were singing the strange passions and alien visions of the audiences' own culture and history. This was particularly the case with black artists. Chuck Berry, Little Richard, girl groups, Arthur Alexander, as well as the musicians influencing them, were introduced to American audiences by the arrival of The Beatles. When The Beatles first toured in the United States, they were adamant that they did not perform in segregated venues. For them there was a passion and lust, an "ars erotica" if we insist, in American music that drove their own creative talents. While Lingis's discussion of this point refers to biopolitics and disciplinary societies, he wonders if there is a heroic or epic art as a response. In this context Lingis asks, "Where is there a master that could tell?"[12]

John Lennon and Paul McCartney were young masters that could tell. As fans appreciated the roots of their music and heritage, The Beatles fostered subsequent generations of musicians who investigated their own strange feelings and alien lusts. Major popular musicians over generations—Stevie Wonder, The Flaming Lips, U2, Tori Amos, Michael Jackson, Bruce Springsteen, Green Day—have cited The Beatles as being essential to their own artistic directions.

A Musical Event

What happened from 1964 onward is well-known. The Beatles established all sorts of firsts—number one singles, albums, sales, covered songs, stadium-sized audiences. They are credited with inventing the rock and roll album, integrating ever new sounds into standard rock music, and whenever there is a list by *Rolling Stone* magazine updating the greatest rock albums of all time, The Beatles still have five in the top 15, including *Sgt. Pepper's Lonely Hearts Club Band* as the perennial number one.

Alain Badiou dismisses any significance of them as an event in popular music. "The Beatles were innovatory, in terms of music or entertainment, only because they plundered forms of serious music, going back to Bach."[13] This pejorative dismissal undermines Badious's own efforts to establish and convey seriousness to an event.

First, the charge of "plundered" betrays an ignorance of Lennon and McCartney's overt indebtedness to their predecessors. They openly worshiped, not plundered, the sources of their shared passions and visions introduced by the pioneers and sources of their own paths. From Badiou's perspective, one might as well accuse Bach of plundering the music of Vivaldi, or Mendelssohn plundering a Bach cantata for his Reformation Symphony.

Second, no one was more serious about music than the 17-year-old John Lennon and 15-year-old Paul McCartney when they met at a church parking lot. Years and decades later, their music has been taken seriously by generations of human beings still enjoying and creating sounds in the shadow of The Beatles. Badiou asserts that an event is "something that brings to light a possibility that was invisible or even unthinkable."[14] Nothing in the early 1960s was more unthinkable than The Beatles.

An existential genealogical approach as found in the writings of Lingis, Lennon/McCartney and The Beatles is more than just a rock band that sold lots of records and developed a legacy lasting generations. There was the initial encounter, a shared recognition of passions and visions, unpredictable moments and a committed project in which one's sense of individual self was subsumed by the intensity of the project and the delirium of their fans. The ecstatic moments Lingis describes at sacred temples, rituals, ceremonies and events in remote parts of the world clearly apply to the prehistorical elements of the Lennon/McCartney confluence.

The Beatles were pioneers in music that generated a way of thinking and being. Contrary to Badiou's myopic disregard, rock and roll critic Greil Marcus claims "The Beatles event... affected not only the feel but the quality of life. They deepened it, sharpened it, brightened it, not merely as a factor in the culture scheme, but as a presence."[15]

Notes

1. Lingis, *The First Person Singular*, 79.
2. Mark Lewisohn, *The Beatles: All These Years; Vol. 1: Tune In* (New York: Crown/Random House, 2013), 224.
3. Ibid., 370.
4. *Backbeat*, a 1994 film directed by Iain Softley. This has also been presented as a stage performance. Its focus is on the first two visits by The Beatles to Hamburg. The central drama is the friendship of John and Stuart Sutcliffe, and then the love between Stu and Astrid Kirschner. The reenactments of the young band playing in the bedlam of Hamburg's Reeperbahn provide a picture of what biographers have described as The Beatles playing punk music before the term "punk music"

was invented. Paul McCartney was disappointed in some of the inaccuracies of the film, such as having John sing lead on "Long Tall Sally" when that was actually one of Paul's covers. George Harrison did not like it at all.

5. Lewisohn, *The Beatles,*392.

6. Bob Spitz, *The Beatles: The Biography* (New York: Little, Brown and Company, 2005), 10. Spitz's epigraph to this work comes from Plato: "When the mode of the music changes, the walls of the city shake."

7. Lewisohn, *The Beatles,* 418-419.

8. Lingis, *Trust,* 63. Obviously, one cannot say too much about the unknown without getting caught in the trap of claiming to know it. In an indirect sense, writes Lingis, the unknown "unleashes the exhilarated thrust, the ecstasy of thought. Is it really true that this ecstasy is a premonition of the final serenity, when the unknown has become a conquered land?" Bewilderment, laughter and fascination fuel an attraction to the unknown. See, Alphonso Lingis, "The Misunderstanding", *Parallax* 4 (1997), 83.

9. Joshua Wolf Shenk, *Powers of Two: Finding the Essence of Innovation in Creative Pairs* (New York: Houghton Mifflin Harcourt Publishing Company, 2014), 59. One of his epigraphs also comes from a philosopher, Martin Buber: "The world is not comprehensible, but it is embraceable: through the embracing of one of its beings."

10. Lewisohn, 625.

11. Lingis, *Foreign Bodies,* 70-71.

12. Ibid., 73.

13. Alain Badiou, *Philosophy and the Event,* trans. Louise Burchill (Cambridge: Polity Press, 2013), 80.

14. Ibid., 9.

15. Greil Marcus, "The Beatles", from *The Rolling Stone History of Rock and Roll* (New York: Random House, 2nd Ed, 2007), 216.

Chapter Eleven

Basketball's Original Magic Show: A Young Master

In winter of 1966-67, the Whitaker Field House of Winston-Salem State College gained an unexpected surge in attendance. Standing-room-only crowds became typical as fans arrived from all corners of the North Carolina area. And they arrived early. Unlike most college basketball games in the 1960s, when fans strolled in as play got underway and still found a decent seat, at Whitaker they filled the stands 30 minutes before the players walked onto the courts for warm-ups.

Fans were buzzing. They eagerly anticipated the latest basketball sensation, Earl Monroe. What was his number? How tall was he? Where did you hear about him? Do you think he'll score 50 points again tonight? were questions that fed the din. Time permitting, they shared stories on their efforts through the wintry weather. Some came by Greyhound bus or local train; others took a cab or bunched up in a friend's car.

One elderly man drove 7 hours to see the sensation in person. His life dated back almost to 1891 when basketball was born in a Massachusetts YMCA. The old-timer's family and friends must have scoffed when he announced his 2-day venture. He had seen it all, they figured. In a world without camcorders, cable television, satellite dishes and all-day TV reruns of games and sports highlights, they were right. The man had seen it all...until Earl Monroe. He said as much when after the game he asked the collegiate star for an autograph.

The announcer for Southwest Missouri State, whose Bears faced Winston-Salem's Rams for the NCAA Division II Championship, interspersed his play-by-play telecast with praise for Monroe's talents as startling and unprecedented. A

Philadelphia native took his young son for a late winter drive to Ohio to see the visiting Rams face Akron. It might be the only time the kid would ever see Monroe in action.

Such travails became the stuff of legends. An elderly man and hordes of fellow basketball fans would have endured many more obstacles in order to testify about the fantastic stories being told and retold of this young master who devised an original way of playing a game they all loved. This phenomenon occurred in the unlikeliest of places—Winston-Salem, a small teacher's college surrounded by basketball goliaths such as Wake Forest, Duke and North Carolina and NC State. Basketball aficionados had to witness for themselves: could anyone really be that good?

As teams began their pre-game drills, many spectators were still unsure of who Monroe was. Standing a slender 6' 3" and walking knock-kneed, he lacked an imposing physical presence. To the casual observer, he was just another player taking practice shots.

Within a minute after the opening tip-off, everyone knew. Suddenly all eyes in Whitaker were drawn to the motions of a player whose body and soul seemingly landed from another realm. Monroe was not a leaper, yet his floating fall-away jumpers defied gravity. His passes arrived at angles that befuddled opponents as well as his own teammates. He slithered between opposing players and eluded double-coverage with head fakes and sleight-of-hand maneuvers. He practically deserved a patent for his inventive dribbling. Monroe's hands cradled a leather ball with a 291/2" circumference so furtively that frustrated referees gave up trying to determine whether it constituted a palming or double dribble violation. Gradually ignored, the basic rules about proper dribbling were forever changed.

Monroe had a knack for getting crowds to expect something new. He might catch opponents by surprise and suddenly dart to the offensive boards, daring the other team's big men to stop him in close. At times his legs and arms could twist in herky-jerky fashion—as if pulled by a puppeteer—and then his moves could just as easily stun opponents and audiences with the grace of whirling dervishes and the fury of ecstatic dancers.

All of this fueled the crowd's fascination. In addition, rumors circulated through the stands that Earl Monroe went by other names. In his hometown Philadelphia, the basketball Mecca of the 1960s, people were known to call him Slick, Savior or Black Jesus. His most publicized nickname, Earl the Pearl, was bestowed by the press only during his senior year.

To his fans and teammates, he was always Magic.

The Sorcerer as Apprentice

The art of magic has long been part of human society. As the harbinger of great dreams and the instigator to dashed hopes, it thrives in a world of mysterious forces. Magic shares etymological roots with magi, those nomads whose gifts were praised as cures and marvels by some or suspected by others to be the work of illusion or chicanery. Ambrosian monk Francesco Guazzo distinguished in 1608 a good and natural magic from a malevolent and destructive one. The former speaks of God's wonders; the latter reflects the Devil's sinister tricks. Practitioners of magic have been persecuted for their blasphemous deeds and curses as frequently as they have been solicited for their daring marvels and miracles.

Houdini, the world's most renowned magician, held public spectacles with his death-defying acts by hanging from bridges or escaping from submerged caskets. After his mother died, the grief-stricken magician attempted to contact her through spiritual mediums. He quickly became skeptical. Despite a friend's (Sir Arthur Canon Doyle) commitment to séances, Houdini used his expertise to expose the frauds of conjurers who promised—and exploited—those people mourning the death of a loved one and wishing to regain contact in the spiritual realm.

To prevent this sort of danger, magicians, like most humans, need a guide. For the powers of magic are capable of corrupting its practitioners. They must first find others to teach them how to perfect the craft, when and how to perform it. Every aspiring young master, including the sorcerer, must start as an apprentice.

Earl Monroe's guide was Clarence "Big House" Gaines, coach of the Winston-Salem Rams. Head of the athletic department, former football star at Morgan State in Baltimore, Maryland, and one of the most successful college basketball coaches of all time, Gaines was an essential figure to young black men for nearly a half century. He invited them to his home, checked on their academic progress and kept contact with their families. He was most proud that over 80 percent of his players graduated college to become teachers, counselors, civic officials and contributors to the public good.

Gaines first met Monroe when Monroe arrived by train from Philadelphia with his life-long buddy, Steve Smith. Coaches in 1960s Division II schools were allotted little travel money to recruit high school prospects. Seldom could they travel a weekend out of state to meet recruits. Occasionally Gaines combined a short vacation in the northeast with scouting the school yards. More often he had trusted alumni, associates and acquaintances to recommend potential college players.

One unofficial scout was Leon Whitley, a former Ram and enduring presence on the Philadelphia courts. He surveyed and scrimmaged with prospects playing in the schoolyards. Whitley was enthralled by Monroe's performances in high school competition as well as in the famed Baker League, a Philadelphia summer league in which college and NBA players kept in shape during the off season. For neighborhood kids unable to afford tickets to Philadelphia's pro team, the 76ers, opportunities to watch Billy Cunningham, Mad Dog Carter, Chink Scott, Wally Jones, Walt Hazzard, Hal Greer, Chet The Jet Walker, among many other local luminaries, were a special treat.

It was at a Baker League game in 1966, during a hot summer

evening at the Bright Hope Baptist Church, where witnesses still testify to an unforgettable event. Before 750 spectators packed into a gym without air conditioning, Bill Bradley, Princeton star and Rhodes Scholar, sank 18 footers and looping hook shots to spark the audience's attention. Then, midway through the first quarter, Monroe arrived at the gym. Stepping his way through the crowd, the buzz started to swell. Are you sure you saw him? Is he here to play? Where's Magic?

Monroe quickly entered the game and, recalls his life-long friend Ted Blunt, the "building went bananas." The crowd hoped for another show. Over the next three quarters, two future hall-of-famers delivered the devotees an unforgettable shootout. From every corner of the court, with long jumpers and fade aways, driving spins and twisting lay-ups, the two stars burned the nets for some 120 points. Monroe scored in the 60s while Bradley hit the upper 50s. Which team won hardly mattered, as fans witnessed an awesome display of marksmanship.

This kind of scene gave Big House Gaines (only his mother called him Clarence) reasons to worry: were Monroe's talents limited to street ball? Fancy moves, trick passes and entertaining shots were fine for playground games, since they entertained players and bystanders. Showboating, however, contributed little to a team's competitiveness. Worse still, a flashy player could get attached to the playground climate and refuse to dream beyond it. Many young men, Coach feared, would not realize that their basketball talents, though short of NBA quality, could with proper coaching still lead to a solid education and a hopeful future. Big House Gaines' career was geared toward that realization.

He found in Monroe a kid who knew little beyond the Philadelphia inner city. Quick tempered, he once ran away to Baltimore for a day. Gangs, grudges and the grit of the streets were part of Monroe's life. During high school he commuted an extra hour in order to avoid one gang's control of hostile intersections that were in his direct path. He later acknowledged being unaware of growing up in the ghetto until he moved away. Hearing that Monroe graduated from high school and dropped out of a preliminary college program, Coach Gaines suspected he was comfortable only with street ball and therefore a recruiting risk.

Gaines was more intent on a player capable of either being a team leader or fitting in with the other players. When looking for prospects, he, like most sports coaches and scouts, had an image of the ideal body. This included solid ankles to sustain the sharp turns and high leaps, long fingers for ball control, toned muscles but no excess weight for quickness, and sturdy feet to enhance the variety of movements needed to play on a wooden floor with 94' by 50' dimensions.

Hearing that Monroe averaged 50 points for a 3-week stretch, Whitaker's neophytes envisioned a lesser version of Wilt Chamberlain, the 7'1" scoring machine. Others heard that Monroe could dictate the direction of the game by passing or rebounding, so they envisioned another Oscar Robertson. (In 1961-62, The Big O averaged 30 points, 11 assists and 12 rebounds a game. Today's players are praised for having a rare "triple double," though remarkably Russell Westbrook topped Robertson's feat in the 2016-17 season.) But Chamberlain and Robertson, like Earvin Johnson, Tim Duncan and Michael Jordan, are among the rare players whose athleticism is so remarkable that they exceed a particular model.

A better candidate for emulation is a player who virtually embodies the model. For guards, there is the small and explosive will-o'-wisp type, a player who can drive, pass and score: Bob Cousy, Nate Archibald, Allen Iverson. There is also the scrappy, agile and all-seeing guard—Lenny Wilkens, Kevin Porter, John Stockton—who leads in assists while ready to sink key baskets. And there is the guard who turns his game into a craft that blends determination and diligence on offense as well as on defense. Jerry West (whose image reportedly inspired the NBA logo), Walt Frazier, Steve Nash, Jason Kidd, typify these characteristics.

Every basketball coach dreams for a guard who is a close fit to one of these models. What any coach would give to have the Iverson, the West or the Kidd type. An entire team can be designed according to their respective talents!

Coaches could not scout for the Earl Monroe type. Monroe bore few translatable features. His arthritic knees made him a risk in terms of durability. Though a soccer stand-out at John Bartram high school, his phenomenal reactions concealed a lack of speed; Ted Blunt jokes that he could always top his friend in a footrace. Monroe was so shy (a trait probably costing him thousands of dollars when he signed his first professional contract) that few scouts saw him as the adept floor leader he eventually became. Too, weighing 180 pounds at 6'3", he clearly lacked a muscular framework, unlike many players who worked with weights to prepare for the rugged aspects of competitive basketball. Winston-Salem's first superstar, Cleo Hill, reminded Gaines of a forerunner to the array of athletic skills later exhibited by Michael Jordan, but a first impression of Monroe evoked no such superlatives. Hence his coach humbly admitted that he didn't really discover Earl Monroe but rather stumbled upon him. It was a lesson in chance.

Chance Events

Political disputes in the 1960s often revolved around historical linkages and causal explanations. Patterns, destinies or laws were employed to interpret many contemporary events. Whether the issue involved family structures or rock music, sports or wars, the emergence of television or the decline of community, human events were understood as explicable, predictable, even inevitable, based on larger forces shaped by the past. "Historical inevitability" is the term repeated and mocked in Edward

Albee's biting and insightful play (and movie), *Who's Afraid of Virginia Woolf?*

What happened at Winston-Salem, North Carolina in 1966-67 involved more the play of chance events than the order of laws or patterns. If there were no hangover of segregation in North Carolina, the teacher's college itself would never have been founded. Had colleges and universities in the reputedly more progressive northeastern parts of the country not engaged in their own form of bigotry, Monroe would likely have been offered a scholarship by one of the many basketball powers in the Pennsylvania region. If his temperament were such that he enjoyed the quick money that goes with being a shipping clerk, his basketball sorcery would never have left the concrete courts of Philadelphia's playgrounds. Complaining about his lack of playing time in the freshman year, Monroe might have left Winston-Salem after his freshman year if Coach Gaines neglected to solicit the intervention of Monroe's mother. Had Monroe first visited Winston-Salem before enrolling, he might have politely rescinded his commitment upon realizing that he and his visiting relatives would be forbidden from a local theater.

The history of basketball too is a chronicle of odd turns and unpredictable twists. James Naismith discovered it by accident. There was a ball, a couple of peach baskets and a bunch of guys needing physical exercise less they concern their bodies with more corrupting desires during the long New England winters. While gaining some unexpected popularity, basketball in its early days was by current standards a plodding game. Minimal dribbling, guards walking the ball up the court, no shot clock, offenses anchored to the big men, and a defense bunched around the free-throw lane. Outside shooting was basically a two-handed set. For a considerable time, basketball was easily more popular as a participant than a spectator sport.

It was by chance that legendary coach John McClendon perused the rules of NCAA basketball and noticed that nothing prohibits players from running up and down the court as soon as they gain possession of the ball. Whether by a rebound, turnover or field goal made, the team getting the ball can charge immediately toward its own basket. With McClendon the fast break was born. (In the 1950s Bill Russell, first at University of San Francisco and then with the Boston Celtics, demonstrated the full potential of a fast break team.) Offenses took many more shots. More importantly, this style of play required such agility and speed of players when switching from defense to offense that an increasing number of teams as well as fans took notice.

The effects of McClendon's revolutionary discovery caught the basketball world by surprise. Basketball specialists soon realized that this type of game also demanded of players to be in tougher physical condition. Whether running or defending against the break, starters needed to play a faster and more relentless pace than the coach did in his collegiate days. This grace and strength, combined with athleticism, thus began turning basketball into the dynamic and appealing game fans now watch.

Coach Gaines relished the fast break. To prepare for a 40-minute contest with constant movement, the Rams were subjected to practices so arduous that under today's NCAA climate Coach would be banned. His view was that drills such as running the players hard in the summer with infrequent water breaks toughened their spirits rather than, as currently held, stressed their hearts with the risk of seizures or strokes.

Still, working a fast break takes more than individual skills and conditioning. Teamwork involving all five players on the court becomes more intense. It begins with an outlet pass from the rebounder. The outlet man then looks for one or two teammates hustling across the court, waiting for a give and go, a wide-open 15 footer, or, when the play works to perfection, a lay-up or dunk (temporarily banned in the late 1960s with the arrival of Lew Alcindor). A haphazard fast break can be suicidal.

Teammates confused over each other's cuts and turns produce turnovers and easy points for the opponent.

Executed properly, the fast break is something to behold. It thrives on taking chances. While journalist Leonard Koppett is right that sport seldom mirrors social reality, basketball can be more than just running up and down the hardwood floor with grown men tussling and fussing over the destination of a leather ball. At times the game is life itself. The fast break entices one to learn to relinquish control of every detail. Occasionally one must throw caution to the wind and see what happens. Coach Gaines assumed this approach when he and his aspiring teachers began their 1966-67 championship season.

Revolutions Great and Small

The "greatest" epithet has appeared in an array of categories. Some are self-proclaimed (Muhammed Ali's "I am the greatest" or the braggarts' chant "We're number 1"). Others are declared by experts, scholars and fans. Candidates for this veritable pantheon have spanned popular consciousness, including: generation (World War II, the Boomers), president (Lincoln, Roosevelt), movie (*Citizen Kane*, *The Godfather*), football game (the Colts/Giants sudden death title, a Friday night high school rivalry), sports record (DiMaggio's hitting streak, Marciano never losing), figures of the second millennium (Luther, Jefferson, Einstein), television sit-coms (*All In the Family*, *The Simpsons*), baseball players (The Babe, The Say Hey Kid), or rock album (The Beatles' *Revolver* or *Sgt. Pepper's*).

The Winston-Salem Rams arguably belong in this pantheon. They lost only one game, a conference play-off that likely caught them looking ahead to the nationals. Sometimes condescendingly referred to as the Teachers rather than the Rams, they were underdogs throughout the season; the polls never put them in the top ten. Regardless, they became the first Negro college to win a national title. Skeptics might point out that this was

Division II basketball. In those days, however, this division featured considerable talent, including future NBA stars such as Willis Reed, Walt Frazier and Bob Dandridge. Billy Packer, the television commentator, was an assistant coach for Wake Forest in the mid-1960s. With singular courage, Packer defied North Carolina's rules on segregation to arrange scrimmages between his and the Rams. (He cleverly planned them for Sunday morning, where people who supported these rules were either praying in church or recovering from Saturday night revelries.) Alas, he found his Demon Deacons, who made the NCAA Division I tournament, were hardly a match for the Rams. How many other NCAA basketball champions attained Winston-Salem State College's level of accomplishment?

The case for a greatest ranking could also be made for Monroe. He broke Bevo Francis' single season scoring record by averaging over 41 points a game. His shooting percentage was 60 percent, unheard of for a shooting guard. Though official stats were unevenly kept, reporters noted that Monroe usually had six or seven assists per game. Add in his six or seven rebounds, two or three steals, and Monroe had a hand in almost every point scored by the champion Rams. (Critics might downplay this proposition as a statistical anomaly or the case of weak opposition. Monroe's next year as a rookie in the NBA, however, underscored his substantial contributions to a team. The Baltimore Bullets, with largely the same cast from the year before, improved by 16 games when he joined them. By comparison, the Royals improved by 14 games in the Big O's rookie season, the Knicks by 7 with Frazier, the Lakers by 11 with West, the Bulls by 11 with Jordan, the Lakers by 13 with Johnson.)

The wonders of magic, though, are rarely accounted for in terms of great or greatest. Too often they are simply inadequate to do justice to its vast range. The feats of a magician are better spoken of in terms of marvelous, spectacular, awesome or unforgettable. He is seen as someone who casts a spell, initiates a curse or leaves the audience spellbound. He appears to create something out of nothing. Penn Jillette (the talkative member of Penn & Teller) remarks that a substantive part of magic dwells in the head. It deals with the expectations, mental habits and imaginations of the audience. The magician leaves an audience always asking: How did he do that? Thus witnesses remember being awestruck.

Earl Monroe did that for basketball fans. Sportswriters, regardless of their talent with words, had difficulty portraying his uncanny moves. They, like Southwest Missouri's announcer, compromised the journalist's code of objectivity by using words such as fabulous, fantastic, magnificent and unbelievable to describe his play.

Yet Monroe, Coach Gaines and the 1966-67 Rams did something more than win and entertain. Their powers of magic became a beacon for social change. Winston-Salem, as its hyphen indicates, is a city linked by two smaller towns. Winston, mostly white, was home to wealthy tobacco and textile entrepreneurs; its eastside neighbor Salem was the poorer area, mostly working class and black. Early settlers to the region included Moravians who were seeking a place to freely live by their religious principles. These included both an abhorrence of slavery and a reluctance to endorse integration. This ambivalence exemplified the erratic history of race relations in North Carolina. Like so many locales in the South and throughout the country, Winston-Salem was marked by legal and implicit conventions of segregation.

As stories of Monroe circulated around the city and region, whites who never ventured near the Salem side hesitantly attended the Whitaker Field House. Ten minutes into the game they forgot their nervousness and joined in the raucous cheering for Monroe and the Rams. To accommodate the thousands of unexpected fans, home games soon had to move from Whitaker to Winston-Salem's Memorial Coliseum, which had a 7500 capacity. This phenomenon led Mary Garber, a pioneer in sports journalism who covered Winston-Salem athletics, to conclude that Monroe and Gaines did more for integration there than any politician or entrepreneur.

When Leon Whitley took his son to see the Rams visit Akron for the Mid-East regionals in March 1967, the Zips had a 52-game winning streak at home. Signs in the arena reflected widespread disbelief: "Earl Monroe is just a myth. He can't compare with Sumpthin' Smith" a typical poster proclaimed. The propaganda failed. Monroe scored 49 points to lead the Rams to an 88-80 upset. He offered his usual assortment of twists, dipsy-doodles and sleight-of-hand tricks that left the Zip players dumbfounded. Unlike today's sports fanatics, who tend to see defeat as an opportunity to boo or insult a player, even denigrate his family heritage, the hostile fans in Akron were transformed. When Monroe left the game with a minute to go, they gave him a standing ovation. They knew that anyone who loved basketball could only appreciate such a performance. They were grateful witnesses.

Nowadays critics of the 1960s debate whether that decade was a disappointment, rightly influential, an exercise in self-righteousness or merely another experiment in misguided utopian dreams. They note that radical movements on college campuses—such as Berkeley or Columbia—ultimately dissipated. They contend that where real power lies—in financial districts of large cities, in the hands of global tycoons or lobbyist-driven halls of Congress—little has changed. For them, the great revolution could succeed only if it proceeded under their direction, according to their vision, and evaluated by their decree. Or else it was doomed to fail.

To the contrary: in numerous college field houses—from Norfolk, Virginia to Akron, Ohio and Evansville, Indiana—a small revolution did happen. Beneath the radar of network television, intellectual centers and power elites, people from all corners of society came together in Winston-Salem's east side to be marveled by a young master's style of play never before seen. For them the ideals of the 60s were neither abandoned slogans nor empty pieties. Inside the dimly lit walls of Whitaker Field House in 1966-67, the revolution was realized with a blend of beauty, grace and chance.

This small revolution was not the work of economic policies, religious leaders, arcane treatises or Congressional edicts. It was the work of Magic—the work of Earl Monroe and the Winston-Salem Rams, basketball's original magic show.

Notes

See Clarence E. Gaines (with Clint Johnson), *They Call Me Big House* (Winston-Salem, NC: John E. Blair Publisher, 2004.), see Ch. 14, "I Stumble onto Earl Monroe." Gaines was aware of Billy Packer's attempts to have his all-white Wake Forest teams scrimmage against a talented all-black team, and admired Packer's courage for these efforts. Echoing Winston-Salem's daily sports writer Mary Garber, perhaps the first woman sports journalist in the country, Gaines believed that the city-wide fascination with Monroe and the team confirmed his "theory of sports bringing the races together was working."

For the many changes in rules, strategies and athleticism of early basketball, see Robert W. Peterson, *Cages to Jump Shot: Pro Basketball's Early Years* (New York: Oxford University Press, 1990). Peterson begins with the founder of basketball, James Naismith, who in 1891 wanted an indoor sport for young people during long cold winters in Massachusetts. The game caught on so quickly that within 20 years barnstorming teams and professional leagues were already forming.

Much of the material for this essay was gained from interviews, via phone or in person. Also very helpful were historical details, stories and rare footage of Monroe's games available in the archives of Winston-State University Library as well as news coverage and records from the city's daily newspaper, *The Winston-Salem Journal*, available in the city's public library.

This essay first appeared as a Special Report in *Basketball Times*, 2006.

Part 3
Tomorrow Never Knows

Chapter Twelve

A Humaneness of the Future

*Anyone who manages to experience the history of humanity as a whole as **his own history** will feel in an enormously generalized way all the grief of an invalid who thinks of health, of an old man who thinks of the dreams of his youth, of a lover deprived of his beloved, of the martyr whose ideal is perishing, of the hero on the evening after a battle that has decided nothing but brought him wounds and the loss of his friend. But if one endured, if one **could** endure this immense sum of grief of all kinds while yet being the hero who, as the second day of battle breaks, welcomes the dawn and his fortune, being a person whose horizon encompasses thousands of years past and future, being the heir of all the nobility of all past spirit—an heir with a sense of obligation, the most aristocratic of old nobles and at the same time the first of a new nobility—the like of which no age has yet seen or dreamed of; if one could burden one's soul with all this—the oldest, the newest, losses, hopes, conquests, and the victories of humanity; if one could finally contain all this in one soul and crowd it into a single feeling—this would surely have to result in a happiness that humanity has not known so far: the happiness of a god full of power and love, full of tears and laughter, a happiness that, like the sun in the evening, continually bestows its inexhaustible riches, pouring them into the sea, feeling richest, as the sun does, only when even the poorest fisherman is still rowing with golden oars! This godlike feeling would then be called—humaneness.*

Nietzsche[1]

Expenditure Without Recompense

Section #337 in Nietzsche's *The Gay Science* is the most integral and frequently cited passage to appear in Lingis's work. It is referred to in his earliest and latest writings, regardless of whether the topic is the sun, death, wealth, splendor, divine powers, love or friendship. Though Nietzsche titled section 337 "The 'humaneness' of the future," he does not seem to revive any form of humanism that Sartre and subsequent existentialists sought. Nor does he promulgate a thesis on what counts as human nature, whether rooted in classical thought or more contemporary sciences emerging in his lifetime such as anthropology, psychology or Darwinism.

Lingis takes section #337 as a departure point to understand and explicate what he sees as one of the fundamental forces—expenditure without recompense. This force is largely overlooked or devalued by prevailing theories about human aspirations and purposes. Even adversaries such as capitalism and Marxism share a suspicion about excess and expenditure. Lingis interprets many theories about humans to be guided by an initial orientation to negatives or needs. They assume humans' relations to others and the world are anchored by what we feel we have lost or taken away, or what is missing that would complete our sense of self or society.

The demands for justice as fairness or equal reciprocity are often manifestations of this basic concern that begins with the importance of what people lack—such as basic rights or opportunities for achieving self-respect. Money, power, sex or survival rank high among the intellectual anchors to explain or interpret various aspects of human life that begin with these demands. Even the importance of the gift, usually the exemplar of generosity, has been often analyzed in terms of satisfying short-term or long-term self-interest, maintaining social cohesion or reconciling previous conflicts.

In this light, "excess" is an afterthought, a sign of irrationality, or a cautionary point that undermines or obscures about the basics of what we lack or what we need. How excess becomes expenditure can also be obscure, given the propensity to account for our experiences primarily in terms of value exchange, reciprocity and equality. We know that justice is illuminated as a blind woman rebalancing the scales of right and wrong. We are inundated with images and messages that our individual worth is equivalent to measurable rewards and recognizable satisfactions. Less clear is what expenditure might mean.

Images of Expenditure

So if its definition is elusive, what does expenditure without recompense look like? Consider some sketches from Lingis's descriptions of a sun's energies, youthful exuberance, rituals and festivals, magical incantations and sacrifices, ecstatic visions and friendship.

Stars: His first book introduces the notion of expenditure without recompense in a disjointed sequence. "The Rangda" begins with a photo of a statuette of Sanghyang Widi, the supreme deity of the Balinese. The text opens with a daring letter from Nietzsche to Cosima Wagner. He imagines to Cosima a star that bestowed a certain species with intelligence and the pursuit of knowledge. This turned out to be a gift with troubling side-effects. For these rational animals soon discovered that the knowledge gained turned out to be false, and not worthy of our belief or sacrifices. The species, Nietzsche sardonically concludes, became extinct upon "the death of truth."[2]

Lingis next speculates on the contrast between systems of reason and systems of the sun. With some hyperbole, he contends that systems of reason calculate, estimate, compensate, exchange according to the relative worth of one another. The problems that these systems generate are problems of civilization. These are limited or enclosed systems. Lingis does not insist such systems are wrong or errant. Rather, they are short-sighted.

Suppose we shift the perspective on wealth from laws that conduct civilization and rational exchange to that of the cosmos. In Lingis's words, "Were we to envisage laws of wealth from the universal point of view, we should discover that the first law of a generalized economy of the solar wealth is expenditure without recompense."[3] How else can we understand our sun, a conflagration that emits 3.8×10^{33} ergs/sec. to provide life on this planet?

Ritualist Trances: From this first law comment he reviews several prevailing outlooks of what counts as a rational economy. The Rangda itself is part of a long history with political twists and cultural conflicts. Lingis recounts the contexts of this ritual, temple ceremony and ecstatic theater, going back to its beginnings in the eleventh century with conflicts over queen, prince, Javanese and Balinese. He notes that "the Rangda is religiously identified with Durga the Inaccessible, dark side of the spouse of Shiva."[4] He summarizes how the Dutch, as part of the rational economy, invaded the area in the early 1800s, and once slaughtered an entire village of some 3600 Balinese.

Then an elaborate description of a moment in an economy of trance is provided. Lingis depicts the instruments and penetrating sounds, the richly colored clothes and masks, jeweled daggers and bloodied throats of birds from a ritual sacrifice. In his words, "Magical incantations circulate, strident and insistent; men begin to turn into gongs, cymbals, insects, demons. From time to time hoarse cries, like the vices of men thousands of years old, are heard."[5]

Yet there is actually very little bloodshed and destruction, certainly a lot less than the average big city commuter traffic, daily murders and the violence the world's technopoles thrust upon one another. The trances induced by the participants in this theatrical ceremony extend to the spectators, "even the children are brought there, and they laugh, entranced or demented themselves, happy, never happier, with a happiness beyond the pleasure their uninhibited everyday sensuality brings flush to their face...happy with an inhuman happiness, perhaps that Nietzsche invoked, 'a God's happiness, full of power and love, full of tears...'"[6] And we rational animals, we television watchers and fearful creatures, Lingis adds, can only see such trances as exercises in superstition or mythical delusions.

Senses of History: Excess also arises in humanity's relation to its own history. Does any other animal bother with the works and failures of its distant ancestors? Surely no sensible creature would fret over how future generations will respect one's legacy. Despite Santayana's frequently cited quip about those who do not learn from the past being condemned to repeat it, there is hardly a universal consensus to the belief that individuals or a species is better off because they debate, appreciate, condemn or even recognize their own history, not to mention the histories of other peoples and species.

In contrast to Hegelian or Christian approaches to history, Lingis turns to Nietzsche for an alternate approach. Rather than a dialectical or purposeful view, Lingis identifies an approach that awaits or creates new possibilities and looks to moments of intensity and rebirth. In this light, he writes, "The historical sense is the highest form of our spirit; it is our participationist ritual, our orgy and our form of ecstasy. It is our means for enduring pure nature."[7] This relation to history is an essential trait of humanity, but as individual forces and strong passions rather than an abstraction or unifying principle. To support the points behind this view, Lingis twice cites section #337 in order to highlight the godlike feeling and comprehensive soul that is experienced as a bestowing of riches that stir laughter, tears, joy and sorrow among humans.

Spectacles and Theaters: The preparation for war, or at least the theatrical representation of it in the Mount Hagen Show in Papua New Guinea, is another manifestation of expenditure. Lingis traces its beginnings to 1964, a carnival in the far east to parallel the one in Rio. When the Highlands Papuans were discovered in 1930, scholars felt they discovered an untainted and precivilized world of savages. Groups or tribes dwelled in the valleys, each having its own language.

The Australian government decided to regulate and minimize the battles and animosities between the tribes, not to mention wanting safe access to all the natural resources (including gold, silver, oil, natural gas) found in these highland valleys. The Mount Hagen shows began as sort of a compromise that allowed the tribes to have a festival while the government could publicize the cessation of war and generate a possible new tourist attraction.

Nevertheless, the show itself still prevails as Lingis's details are introduced by citing #337. Participants embody the passions of their ancestors, be it grief, honor, betrayal, courage or hope. From Lingis's perspective, "The men and women marching, dancing, filling the air with cries and chants under Mount Hagen, are splendid with the nacreous shells of mollusks, the skeletons and fangs of serpents, the tusks of boars, the teeth of flying foxes, the plumes of birds." Such excesses elude the interpretations of Darwin, Freud or Marx. Their ideas for explaining such phenomena as the Mount Hagen Show prevent them from seeing the shows as expenditures of splendor and joy without recompense.[8]

Friendships: As we revisit "Cargo Cult", Lingis asks if there exists a law that dictated Gopal to choose the American traveler to be a friend. The law could be ethical, political, evolutionary in basis, yet none could explain or justify the ephemeral friendships encountered in India. His reflections on friendship follow the discussion on how Aristotle and many of us see "all social existence to be an exchange of complementary values." [9] #337 is then quoted, followed by his befriending Devika and Arun. They take him to see cobra venom feeding the fix of addicts and floating ambers of recently burnt corpses. Lingis meets Gopal Hardilay, who introduces Lingis to an orgy of sensations in his hometown by the Ganges. Gopal brings him to hear the bells ring for the goddess, smell the fires of incense and animal sacrifices, feel the motions of the elephants leading a bridal procession, taste the dirt and sweat of crowded city alleys and streets, be moved by silent nights and hissing monkeys.

Lingis considers making some photos of Gopal as a gift. The originals did not turn out, all blank. Weeks later he returns to Gopal's town in the hope of taking more photos so he can give them to Gopal. Without warning, Gopal places in Lingis's hand a tiny silver statue, then ancient Tibetan coins he found in the river. Immediately Lingis admits this is no friendship of complementary values. "...if I gave you all the possessions I had it would not be the equivalent, since I have a job and more salary comes in, automatically, each month, with pension till I die."[10]

It was the orphan boy, not the college professor, who had given everything he had in the name of friendship. And it was the professor who here was the recipient of expenditure without recompense.

Truthful States: In Argentina Lingis by chance finds *Aconcagua*, a book by psychotherapist Juan Aguilar. One of his patients, Miguel, leads an enviable life. Educated, solid family life, financially sound with a profitable real estate career, clearly he seems to be the last one who needs a shrink. Yet Miguel found no meaning to his accomplishments. He "has" a good job, "has" a wife and good kids, "has" all the material necessities and more. But what do they all mean?

The therapist did not offer any counseling or medications, only to recommend that Miguel climb a mountain, Cerro Aconcagua, the highest in the Americas. It is a dangerous climb, with wind chills dipping into 80 degrees below, difficult terrain and the ever-present threats of avalanches or ice storms. It takes 4 months of physical and dietary discipline to prepare for the ascent. And the therapist offered to accompany his patient on this venture, without pay. Risking their lives for one another, they reached the point where in 2 days they could step upon the summit. The thin air, the cold, whiteout winds and ice were too much and finally thwarted their efforts, forcing them to quickly return to the base camp.

Lingis is struck by this story. The meaning of life is one of philosophy's perennial concerns, even if no agreement has been settled. The therapist did not even address the likely etiologies of the patient's worries, just that he abandon his way of life and try the unusual, leap into the unknown and climb a mountain that has brought death to even the most experienced climbers. Doesn't this experience recall our knowledge of the passions, transgressions, the clarity or inherent obscurity of the meaning of our lives, and whether it is even attainable?

His response is that the passions convey a knowledge that functions differently than the way objective observation gains knowledge. Lingis's example implies many passions seek the enigma rather than certainty, such as of a beloved. He writes, "We think we do not know a woman until we have melted before her kindness and feared her wrath, been anguished before her vulnerability and retreated before her power, been illuminated by her insights and charmed by her foolishness, until she has made us laugh as we have never laughed, made us weep in misery."[11] This is supported with a lengthy quote from #337.

Lingis sees #337 as expenditure that emerges from the gods, nature and humanity—from divine spirits and sacred moments, from animals and landscapes, from works and monuments, among many others. The happiness of tomorrow's humanity, though, is not found in self-realization, social utopia, great power or wealth. For Nietzsche this happiness culminates in "the most truthful state." In Lingis's view, the meaning of life sought by the patient can be found in saying "Yes to all that is and happens, loving one's life, loving life loving the world. We must trust our joy, for joy is the most truthful state."[12]

A Fisherman with Golden Oars

The sections following #337 provide glimpses of Nietzsche's own possible takes on a humaneness of the future. #338 envisions a life where the religion of pity has disappeared and humans learn to share joy rather than suffering. #339, "Vita femina", calls for new encounters and unveilings of beauty, be it "a work, a deed, humanity, or nature..." #340, "The dying Socrates," invokes Nietzsche's admiration for Socrates while eschewing any nostalgia or a return to the ancient Greeks. Perhaps the courage or silence of Socrates can be reborn in a future humanity, but without his final words of malice toward life. Next section, "The Greatest Weight", introduces the eternal recurrence, with the response being immense anxiety in the possibility of living this exact life again and again or, in Nietzsche's words, a sign of "how well disposed would you have to become to yourself and to life *to crave nothing more fervently* than its ultimate eternal confirmation and seal?"

The last section closed the first edition of *The Gay Science*. It introduces Zarathustra, the central figure of Nietzsche's next book. Zarathustra wants to end his 10 years of solitude and be a man again, be among humans again. Zarathustra is overflowing with energy, wisdom and insights. He speaks in terms of expenditure without recompense. But to do this Zarathustra also needs "hands outstretched to receive it. I want to give away and distribute until the wise among men enjoy their folly once again and the poor their riches."[13]

Excess becomes expenditure without recompense when there are hands to receive it. In the words of Lingis, these hands can also be extended to our eyes, ears, faces and bodies, hearts and souls. That is why the image of the "poorest fisherman rowing with golden oars" is the most enduring image in Lingis's writings. It completes the experience of expenditure. And as seen in the photos and descriptions of individuals he has met, Lingis has often been the grateful recipient of such expenditure.

At one time or another most of us have been fortunate or unexpected recipients of another's expenditure. At one time or another you or I have likely expended our thoughts, kindness and creativity without recompense, even unaware what joy or insight it brought to someone else. "Happiness consists in knowing that we live by luck and in the reckless freedom of staking our life,"[14] Lingis observes about so many human experiences. Studying these experiences and their backgrounds has been a central task in Lingis's philosophical story-telling and existential genealogy.

Whether retelling and reflecting on the early days of a preeminent rock band or electrifying basketball player, rebels in oppressive regimes, vagabonds in destitute neighborhoods, lovers in prison, nomads in their camps, orphans in third world countries, among so many others, the writings of Alphonso Lingis present a direction for us to address chance face-to-face encounters, unexpected passions and sacred visions, projects abandoned or accomplished and lived moralities in distant lands and times. No doubt his writings can draw some dismal, dark and debilitating insights into our own species.

Yet his work also risks moments of happiness, trust and joy that embody the aspirations of all philosophy—the most truthful state.

Notes

1. Nietzsche, *The Gay Science,* #337.
2. Lingis, *Excesses,* 71.
3. Ibid., 72.
4. Ibid., 77.
5. Ibid., 78.
6. Ibid., 80.
7. Lingis, *Deathbound Subjectivity,* 77.
8. Lingis, *Violence and Splendor,* 146-147.
9. Lingis, *Excesses,*148-149.
10. Ibid., 162.
11. Alphonso Lingis, "Aconcagua", in *Passion in Philosophy,* ed.

Randolph C. Wheeler (Lanham: Lexington Books, 2017), 12.

12. Ibid., 13.

13. Nietzsche, *The Gay Science,* #342.

14. Lingis, *Body Transformations,* 144.

Index

zero
books

CULTURE, SOCIETY & POLITICS

Contemporary culture has eliminated the concept and public figure of the intellectual. A cretinous anti-intellectualism presides, cheer-led by hacks in the pay of multinational corporations who reassure their bored readers that there is no need to rouse themselves from their stupor. Zer0 Books knows that another kind of discourse – intellectual without being academic, popular without being populist – is not only possible: it is already flourishing. Zer0 is convinced that in the unthinking, blandly consensual culture in which we live, critical and engaged theoretical reflection is more important than ever before.

If you have enjoyed this book, why not tell other readers by posting a review on your preferred book site.

Recent bestsellers from Zero Books are:

In the Dust of This Planet
Horror of Philosophy vol. 1
Eugene Thacker
In the first of a series of three books on the Horror of
Philosophy, *In the Dust of This Planet* offers the genre of horror
as a way of thinking about the unthinkable.
Paperback: 978-1-84694-676-9 ebook: 978-1-78099-010-1

Capitalist Realism
Is there no alternative?
Mark Fisher
An analysis of the ways in which capitalism has presented itself
as the only realistic political-economic system.
Paperback: 978-1-84694-317-1 ebook: 978-1-78099-734-6

Rebel Rebel
Chris O'Leary
David Bowie: every single song. Everything you want to know,
everything you didn't know.
Paperback: 978-1-78099-244-0 ebook: 978-1-78099-713-1

Cartographies of the Absolute
Alberto Toscano, Jeff Kinkle
An aesthetics of the economy for the twenty-first century.
Paperback: 978-1-78099-275-4 ebook: 978-1-78279-973-3

Malign Velocities
Accelerationism and Capitalism
Benjamin Noys
Long listed for the Bread and Roses Prize 2015, *Malign
Velocities* argues against the need for speed, tracking
acceleration as the symptom of the ongoing crises of capitalism.
Paperback: 978-1-78279-300-7 ebook: 978-1-78279-299-4

Meat Market
Female Flesh under Capitalism
Laurie Penny
A feminist dissection of women's bodies as the fleshy fulcrum
of capitalist cannibalism, whereby women are both consumers
and consumed.
Paperback: 978-1-84694-521-2 ebook: 978-1-84694-782-7

Poor but Sexy
Culture Clashes in Europe East and West
Agata Pyzik
How the East stayed East and the West stayed West.
Paperback: 978-1-78099-394-2 ebook: 978-1-78099-395-9

Romeo and Juliet in Palestine
Teaching Under Occupation
Tom Sperlinger
Life in the West Bank, the nature of pedagogy and the role of a
university under occupation.
Paperback: 978-1-78279-637-4 ebook: 978-1-78279-636-7

Sweetening the Pill
or How we Got Hooked on Hormonal Birth Control
Holly Grigg-Spall
Has contraception liberated or oppressed women? *Sweetening the Pill* breaks the silence on the dark side of hormonal contraception.
Paperback: 978-1-78099-607-3 ebook: 978-1-78099-608-0

Why Are We The Good Guys?
Reclaiming your Mind from the Delusions of Propaganda
David Cromwell
A provocative challenge to the standard ideology that Western power is a benevolent force in the world.
Paperback: 978-1-78099-365-2 ebook: 978-1-78099-366-9

Readers of ebooks can buy or view any of these bestsellers by clicking on the live link in the title. Most titles are published in paperback and as an ebook. Paperbacks are available in traditional bookshops. Both print and ebook formats are available online.

Find more titles and sign up to our readers' newsletter at http://www.johnhuntpublishing.com/culture-and-politics

Follow us on Facebook
at https://www.facebook.com/ZeroBooks

and Twitter at https://twitter.com/Zer0Books